ELGIN

A History of Elgin, Texas 1872 - 1972

COMPILED BY

MEMBERS OF THE ELGIN HISTORICAL COMMITTEE

Published By NorTex Press
An Imprint of Wild Horse Media Group
P.O. Box 331779
Fort Worth, Texas 76163
1-817-344-7036
www.WildHorseMedia.com

Paperback 978-1-68179-380-1
Hardback 978-1-68179-467-9

DEDICATION

This book became a reality largely because one zealous Elgin woman had the foresight to begin more than a year ago to think Elgin Centennial and to sort through her extensive files for suitable material to be in readiness for the publishing of a history of Elgin in 1972.

To Emma S. Webb (Mrs. C. W.) this book is lovingly dedicated in appreciation of her dream to perpetuate the early development, growth and progress of Elgin through the past one hundred years and who so graciously lay aside her duties as a practicing attorney to write portions of the history, to meet with the cooperative compilers, to encourage and share information, and throughout her residency in Elgin has always been willing to sponsor and to earnestly work for any project that would promote the betterment of Elgin.

PREFACE

The Historical Committee, in writing this Centennial Book, has endeavored to collect and compile some of the history of Elgin through its first one hundred years.

We are especially indebted to the *Elgin Courier*, the local newspaper. Without being permitted the research of its old newspaper files, this book would have been almost impossible. We have searched through Bastrop County records; written letters to various departments, organizations, and individuals asking for help and information; and interviewed many of our older citizens and others, who have furnished information and loaned their early day photographs to be printed in this book.

We are grateful to those who have made possible the printing of this book and added greatly to its historical interest through advertisements.

To everyone who has helped in any way, we wish to express our deepest appreciation.

THE ELGIN HISTORICAL COMMITTEE

Mrs. C. W. Webb
Mrs. Syd Davis
Donald Whitten
Mrs. Jesse C. Miller
Mr. and Mrs. Leo Foehner
Miss Fairbanks Westbrook
Mr. and Mrs. Noel Branton
Mrs. Jarmon Wiley

PREFACE
2002

The History Book Committee of the Elgin Historical Association is reprinting this wonderful, original "Elgin…A History of Elgin, Texas 1872-1972" in conjunction with the Grand Opening of the Elgin Union Depot Museum. We have added some current information about Elgin and the area, along with a few corrections. We are in the middle of a growth spurt for communities east of Austin as our population numbers show. In 1990, the population of Elgin was 4,684. In the year 2000, it had risen to 5,700. Although the location of new residents and business to the community will press forward, the heart and history of Elgin remains as a cattle and farming community, a way of life which will forever be our legacy.

We submit to the community of today and for years to come this information with our heartfelt appreciation for the generosity of spirit and information as we publish this book in conjunction with the opening of the Union Depot Museum of Elgin on June 1, 2002. As President of the Elgin Historical Association, Charlene Hanson Jordan has spearheaded the renovation and completion of the old passenger depot into a building of beauty and integrity for Elgin's first museum and archives. Gregory Free was the historical architect. Eric Carlson has been the mayor of Elgin during this period.
Special appreciation to Tom Eisenhour.

THE ELGIN HISTORY BOOK COMMITTEE

Donald Whitten, member, Centennial Book Committee
Donna Lundgren Snowden
Zoe Webb
Sandy Murphree

THE ELGIN HISTORICAL ASSOCIATION

SPECIAL APPRECIATION

Elwanda Lundgren
Nell Davis, member, Centennial Book Committee
Betty Lynn Meyer
Jack Webb

June 2002

TABLE OF CONTENTS

I EARLY LAND GRANTS

The history of Elgin goes back to Stephen F. Austin's "Little Colony". In 1832, Thomas Christian and Jonathan Burleson, members of Austin's Colony, received grants of land from the Mexican Government. Thomas Christian received a league of land situated to the east of the north east of the Colorado River and about six leagues north of the then new town of Bastrop. Jonathan Burleson received a quarter-league of land adjoining the Thomas Christian grant. The City of Elgin now stands on a portion of each of these grants.

Jonathan Burleson came to Texas in 1830 with his father, James Burleson, and several brothers, one of which was General Edward Burleson. Jonathan never lived on his grant, settling instead on his mother's-in-law league west of the river in Bastrop. During the Texas Revolution, he fought in the Battles of Velasco, Gonzales, Bexar and San Jacinto.

Thomas Christian, with his wife, Mary Buchanan Christian, and five small children, came to Texas with the last contingent of Austin's "Little Colony." They reached Bastrop in May of 1832, remaining there until after Sepetmber 11, 1832, when their youngest child, Sarah Buchanan, was born. Because of warlike conditions of the Indians in the area of the Christian grant, they did not move to it; but rather moved to Mr. Webber's place on the Colorado River. In August of 1833, Christian was killed by Indians during the Wilbarger Episode. The following year Mrs. Christian married James Burleson and was widowed again in 1836 after the addition of another little girl to the family.

The young widow and her family became participants in the drama of the Texas Revolution. As General Sam Houston led his army of Texians in a strategic retreat toward San Jacinto, word reached Bastrop that Mexican troops were headed for the area. Mrs. Christian and her seven children joined area settlers in the "Runaway Scrape" to Washington-on-the-Brazos.

In 1840, Mrs. Christian-Burleson and her children moved to the Christian league. She built a log cabin which was located among the trees across from the present location of the New Century Club. This was the first house in what later became a part of the town of Elgin. Her nearest neighbor was Mike Young, some three miles south. In 1847, she built a conventional Texas ranch house nearer the edge of the prairie, with two large rooms and an open hall between. In 1855, she added two other rooms and weather boarded it. This house now stands at the intersection of Lexington Road and Louise Street. Some changes have been made, but most of the original lumber holds the house together. The long porch that extended across the front of the house was enclosed for additional room and a smaller end porch has been added.

There are two little stories of local color during Mrs. Christian-Burleson's residence on this grant which have come down to us. While she and her seven children were living in the log cabin, the settlers were warned of a threatened Indian raid. She was busy getting a piece of cloth out of the loom, so did not heed the warning until rather late in the afternoon. When she took the cloth from the loom, she and her children escaped, some riding a horse and some in an ox cart. They got as far as the nearest neighbor's place that night, and discovering that the log chain had been lost, she sent her son, John, and a Negro boy back the next morning to look for it. They found the house had been raided, the feather beds opened and feathers scattered to the breeze. Everything was topsy-turvy. The family hurried on to Bastrop where the settlers had been called to flee for safety.

The other incident happened after she had built the larger house on the prairie. Every winter roving Indians came into the neighborhood for the winter season. One day two braves knocked at her back door, and with fear and trembling she opened to see what they wanted. They asked for two beeves; and rejoicing that they wanted nothing more, she told them to take them. The two braves returned the following winter and holding out two buffalo robes explained, "These for the beeves."

The seven children of "Grandma" Burleson, as she came to be called, grew to womanhood, and one son, John, to manhood on this original grant. They married and became leaders in the growth of the community.

"Grandma" Burleson lived in her home on the edge of the prairie until her death in 1870, shortly before the coming of the railroad to this section. As was customary in those early days, each family had its own cemetery on its own land. Mrs. Christian-Burleson was buried in the Christian family cemetery, along with some of her immediate family and other relatives. A chainlink fence, erected by her descendants, now protects this cemetery, located on a wooded knoll a quarter of a mile east of her homestead.

II THE BEGINNING

Railroad building in Texas did not get started until 1851; and even then, such investments were uncertain ventures. A line was built from Houston to Hempstead by 1858; and enterprising citizens from Brenham managed by February, 1860, to get a branch from there to Brenham, which operated on a limited schedule. Further rail construction was suspended by the War between the States.

After the War, the Houston and Texas Central Railroad contracted to build a branch from Brenham to reach Austin by January 1, 1872. The original survey was made to take the route from McDade to the Colorado River valley, toward the more populated region of Webberville and Hornsby Bend, where lumber mills, cotton plantations and farms in established operation had a need for immediate railway facilities, and would have provided a great deal of revenue for the company. A great portion of the surveying had been completed when the flood of 1869 came, with the river rising sixty feet, covering the bottom lands and completely submerging the proposed rail bed. The company then ordered a new survey made, and the route through the present day Elgin and Manor to Austin was adopted.

The road was largely built by convict labor, using wheel barrows and mules to build up much of the dirt work. Professor A. H. Carter, who came to the area in October, 1871, wrote years later that when he drove in an old hack from his rail destination in Giddings to his new location, he observed the activity of the many convicts in the attempt to complete the construction on time. Another oldtimer, Miles Hill, Elgin's first lawyer and founder of the *Elgin Courier,* also wrote that he had many times "seen convicts in stocks, as punishment for their failure to do the work demanded of them"; and that, truly, much suffering resulted in the building of the railroad. The line was completed a few days ahead of schedule, and on Christmas Day, 1871, the first train steamed through what was later to become Elgin and arrived at Austin.

The 1872 *Texas Almanac* listed the stations and their distances from Hempstead as follows:

Hempstead to Paige—71 miles
Hempstead to McDade—82 miles
Hempstead to Glasscock—92 miles
Hempstead to Manor—104 miles
Hempstead to Austin—118 miles

Before a station was established, Glasscock was the flag stop for the present Elgin area and was located about one mile west of the present town, near a large tank where the trains took on water. Another old-timer, Charles Gillespie, said that at that time where Elgin's leading business houses now stand, the wild beast roamed and Mother Earth was covered with cactus, mesquite, and grand old oaks.

The Deed of Dedication from the Rail Directory naming the townsite Elgin is dated August 18, 1872. Bearing the same date, surveyor Theo Kosse's plat placed the train depot in the center of a one-mile square area, which is the location of the present wooden freight depot. John Gordon was the first depot agent.

Elgin was named for Robert Morris Elgin, land commissioner for the Houston and Texas Central Railroad. According to John E. Elgin, nephew of Robert M. Elgin, most of the towns along the line were named for the company's officials or promoters of the road.

Although Robert M. Elgin never lived in the town which bears his name, his is a proud name linked with many outstanding accomplishments. Elgin was born in Smith County, Tennessee, on September 24, 1825. He came to Texas in 1841 with an oxen-drawn wagon train, and settled in Washington County near Brenham where he served as deputy county clerk.

After serving under General Zachary Taylor during the Mexican War, Elgin moved to Austin as chief clerk of the General Land Office. He moved to Houston in 1865 to assume the duties of land commissioner of the Houston and Texas Central Railroad. He left the railroad in 1891 to enter private business.

A member of the Masonic Lodge, Elgin served as Grand Master of the Grand Lodge of Texas and Grand Commander of Knights Templars. He was a faithful member of the Episcopal Church, serving in various capacities. Elgin died on July 9, 1913, and is buried in Glenwood Cemetery in Houston.

Mr. Elgin's nephew stressed the pronunciation of the name, saying, "There is one thing in which I desire to solicit your co-operation, that is, to give the name its proper pronunciation. There are many people who will pronounce the last syllable gin as liquor gin, while the proper pronunciation is as you would pronounce the word begin. We would like in Texas to keep the correct Scotch pronunciation as the family uses it."

Early Houston and Texas Central locomotive.

Robert Morris Elgin.

III PERRYVILLE

The history of Elgin would not be complete without the history of Perryville, or Hogeye as it was nicknamed, located 2½ miles south of the town of Elgin. Many of Elgin's early citizens moved here from Hogeye. The community was called by three different names. The post office was officially named Young's Settlement, and the churches and Masonic Lodge carried the name Perryville. The name Hogeye was given to the stage stop—the Litton home—because it was there that a community dance was held, and the fiddler knew only one tune, called "Hogeye," which he played over and over as the crowd danced on the puncheon floor.

On the roster of Austin's "Little Colony" is the name of Elizabeth Standifer, listed as being a widow and farmer, who came to Texas with her four children, James, William, Jacob, and Sarah. It was on her league that the community of Perryville was established. Sarah Standifer married John Litton, who had come to Texas in 1827. John and Sarah's home, a two-story part log and lumber structure, was also the stage stand where the horses were changed as the old Concord stages plied their way from Houston to the west. John was the first postmaster for Young's Settlement post office, having been appointed November 5, 1849, and the post office was located in his home.

Perryville had twelve to fifteen houses in the settlement. Some of its businesses were a saloon; a general store; a grocery store run by J. B. Scott; a blacksmith shop run by L. P. Eggleston; a store run by John Tom Litton; and a blacksmith shop run by Ben Carter, a former slave, who made and perfected the famous Ben Carter bridle bit. There were four doctors in the community through the years—Doctors Oliver, McPherson, Young and Sheasby—some of whom practiced later in Elgin.

In this area a very interesting business venture was once commenced. After the Civil War, the United States put up as "Government Surplus" the camels which it had shipped into Texas in 1856, where it was hoped such animals could be trained and used as carriers in the arid West. Colonel Bethel Coopwood and Enon Lanfear acquired thirty-two or more of the animals, and they were kept on the Lanfear farm about one mile west of Perryville. These two men tried, unsuccessfully, to use them for public transportation and freighting—mainly, for the mail to San Antonio, Brownsville, and Mexico City. When the venture failed they sold them to fairs and circuses.

With the coming of the railroad just 2½ miles away, the people of Perryville began to move to Elgin. They recognized the business opportunities and took advantage of them. Some who moved to Elgin were J. J. Joplin, who built the first hotel; O. H. P. McGinnis, who built a store; as did R. V. Standifer; J. H. Litton had the first meat market with John Chiles to run it. Dr. Samuel Sheasby moved his office and opened a drug store.

Union Depot Elgin Texas.

Pub. by S. T. Biggs

Union Depot built in 1903.

Sec 11

Houston and Texas Central Railroad section house built in 1884. Located on railroad past oil mill, house was moved only a few years ago. Section Foreman F. M. Atchison and family shown on porch about 1887.

Home of John S. Smith built around 1890 on present location of Sunset Motel. His wife, Sarah, was the daughter of Mrs. Mary Christian-Burleson.

Mrs. M. B. Keeble's private school class, standing in front of her home in 1891.

Elginites awaiting President McKinley's train in 1901.

IV TOWN OF ELGIN

It was May 31, 1873, when the incorporation of the Town of Elgin was approved by the State Legislature. The first officials of Elgin were: R. V. Standifer, Mayor; J. A. Case, Marshall; L. Hellman, B. Harris, James P. Reynolds and L. C. Cunningham, Aldermen.

The first store in Elgin was that of Jake Fetterly—a frame building on which George and G W. Dorris were the carpenters. R. V. Standifer's frame store at the corner of Main and Depot Streets was the second store built. The third was built by Ben Harris. In order to gain the business of more customers, some merchants had wagon yards at the rear of their businesses where the farmers and their families could camp overnight while they did their shopping. These were places where visiting was done among friends whose homes were separated by several miles.

The first saloon in town was built by Bill Calhoun in 1872. It was operated by a Mr. Case and was later known as the Miles Saloon. Peter Burns had a saloon just west of the present O'Conner building, which was also sort of an eating place. Joe Bennett ran a keg saloon. In a keg saloon the customer came in, turned on the faucet in any keg he wished, took his drink, laid his money down, and then went out.

An interesting letter was written from Elgin in 1873 and was signed only by the name "Observer". It was reprinted in the May 30, 1957, *Elgin Courier:*

"Elgin is a new station just east of Austin, on the western branch of the Houston and Texas Central Railway. This railway company paid a heavy price for the land on which the town is located, well knowing that they will be repaid at an early day, many times over what it cost.

Until lately, transportation has been limited to this branch of the railroad. Things are moving faster now. Transportation is now being furnished us. Elgin is beginning to assume the proportions of a town 'not to be sneezed at'. Many lots have been sold. Several buildings are going up where only a dense forest was located.

A large freight-house has been erected . . . I venture to predict that more cotton will be shipped from this point next season than from any depot this side of Brenham. We want more people here to do business. Those who have located here do not keep enough stock on hand. Two or three more lumber yards are needed, for we will have a heavy trade from Milam and Williamson Counties . . . A good hotel is wanted more than anything else in 1873, and we need somebody who knows how to operate it.

Judge L. C. Cunningham, a veteren of early Texas, and his son Captain Cunningham, have established a planing and sawmill in Elgin . . ."

On December 30, 1873, R. V. Standifer bought the property where Luther Lundgren's used car lot is presently located and built a house some time later. This house is still standing but was moved to another location several years ago. In 1877, he bought the lots where the Eltex Theater is now located and built the first brick building there.

Gus Jones owned one of Elgin's first lumber yards. His large home and spacious gardens were supposed to be the most imposing in town at that time. Mr. Jones was responsible for bringing Thomas O'Conner to town as a brick mason to build chimneys for the houses he built. Mr. O'Conner started the brickmaking business here—an industry that was to put Elgin on the map.

By 1890, the population had reached 831, and Elgin was growing. During the next few years many new businesses were started. The construction business, brick making, farming, and nearby coal mines brought many Mexican and Negro citizens to this area.

Its mild temperate climate, with rich black soil on one side and fertile sandy loam on the other, drew many people to the surrounding area. Germans, Swedes and Czechs came in large numbers. They, as well as the farmers already here, developed one of the best farming areas in the state. Cotton, corn and feed crops grew readily and in abundance in the blacklands of the prairie, and the world's finest watermelons, cantaloupes, sweet potatoes, peanuts, tomatoes and all manner of truck crops flourished in the sandy soil.

With Elgin's growth, more rail facilities were desired. Bastrop, sixteen miles to the south, the county seat, also wanted rail advantages. The Missouri, Kansas and Texas Railroad, nicknamed "Katy", had reached Taylor in 1882. In 1885, a group of interested citizens met in Elgin to get underway the building of the Taylor, Elgin and Bastrop Railroad. In 1886, this organization was taken over by the Taylor, Bastrop and Houston Railroad Company, which began the building of the line. That same year the Katy acquired this line and continued the construction on to Houston.

Elgin was greatly benefitted by the excellent railway facilities, being at the junction point of the Missouri, Kansas and Texas and the Houston and Texas Central (later Southern Pacific) lines. For many years, four day and four night passenger trains stopped at Elgin. In 1903, a red brick Union Depot was erected at the intersection of the H & TC and M K &T lines. In 1960, after passenger services were discontinued on both lines, the City of Elgin purchased the depot and it is now used as the local Police Station.

Southside Elgin looking east about 1906.

Southside Elgin looking west in 1907, Roemer Lumber Yard to left, near track; top of red brick hotel above lumber yard; with new Elgin National Bank on corner.

South Main during cotton season in 1912.

Interior of J. F. Meeks' store in early 1900s, located on Southside.

A. J. Miller Confectionery where first can of ice cream made and retailed in Elgin was sold. From left to right: Mrs. Miller; A. J. Miller; Harry Davis, their son; Capt. F. S. Wade.

An early day saloon.

V CITY OF ELGIN

The year 1900 produced a bumper crop of cotton, and a period of prosperity was enjoyed by the citizenship. The population had increased from 831 in 1890 to 1258 in 1900. After the population had passed the one thousand mark it seemed advisable to incorporate the Town of Elgin as the City of Elgin, so an election was held at the building owned by A. S. Christian and known as the front end of the old "Ten Pin Alley". The election was held on September 12, 1901, and there were 149 votes for and 47 against the incorporation. It was then necessary to elect a major, a marshall, and five aldermen for the City of Elgin. This election was held on Thursday, October 10, 1901, and the following officers were elected: Charles Gillespie, Mayor; J. D. Hemphill, Marshall; W. E. McCullough, J. Wed Davis, Ed Lawhon, Max Hirsch, and F. S. Wade, Aldermen.

Law enforcement prior to this time had been under the jurisdiction of Bastrop County officers, but at this time a civil and criminal code was drawn up by Miles H. Hill, the City Attorney. Sam J. Isaacks served as the first City Secretary. One of the first ordinances passed by the city government was that trains must not proceed beyond the speed of ten miles per hour through the city or they would be fined $100.

In 1907, Mr. Gillespie was still Mayor; James Keeble was Treasurer; J. O. Smith was City Secretary; and Glen Jackson, City Marshall. John Sowell was elected Constable in 1906, and for thirty-seven years he served as a peace officer in one capacity or another.

For several years after 1900, the boll weevil hit the cotton crop, and Elgin's growth slowed down. There were only a few businesses on the Northside, and those on the Southside were mainly frame or low brick buildings. By 1906 things were beginning to look up. A building boom started that lasted through 1910. During this period the following buildings were erected: Bassist Opera House, Elgin National Bank (on Southside), Rivers Bros. Merchantile Co., Prewitt Building, Mc-

Clellan Inn, Taylor Building, Oil Mill, Elgin Butler Brick Co., Wilbarger Lumber Co., Merchants and Farmers Bank, and a new school on the Northside. New residential additions to the town were developed—Garrett, Wilson, H. B. Smith, Tingle, Wade and Owens, A. H. Carter Additions—and many new homes were built. This period saw the development of a good water system, an ice factory, and an electric light plant. On the streets of Elgin the automobile had begun to appear, and John Puckett opened a garage.

In 1910, an article in the *Elgin Courier* praised the city fathers for directing the trend of prosperity, reading, "Elgin has prospered under a well-planned and carried out city government, incorporated under the laws of the land and presided over by substantial and competent business men and property owners." The municipal officers at that time were W. H. Kennedy, Mayor; John Sowell, Marshal; J. W. Thomas, Secretary and ex-officio Tax Assessor-Collector; R. Roemer, James Walling, R. L. Carter, Albert Sellstrom and Max Hirsch, Aldermen.

During this period, families from out on the prairie and the surrounding areas moved into Elgin, established businesses and built nice homes. This made a big contribution to the growth and prosperity of the town.

Northside Elgin looking north about 1912.

Northside Elgin looking south in 1908.

Building on site of present Elgin National Bank. Lower floor contained the S. T. Cain Drugstore and office of Dr. Auler. Dr. Hudson had an office upstairs.

N. P. Smith Studio about 1908.

Inside of N. P. Smith Studio.

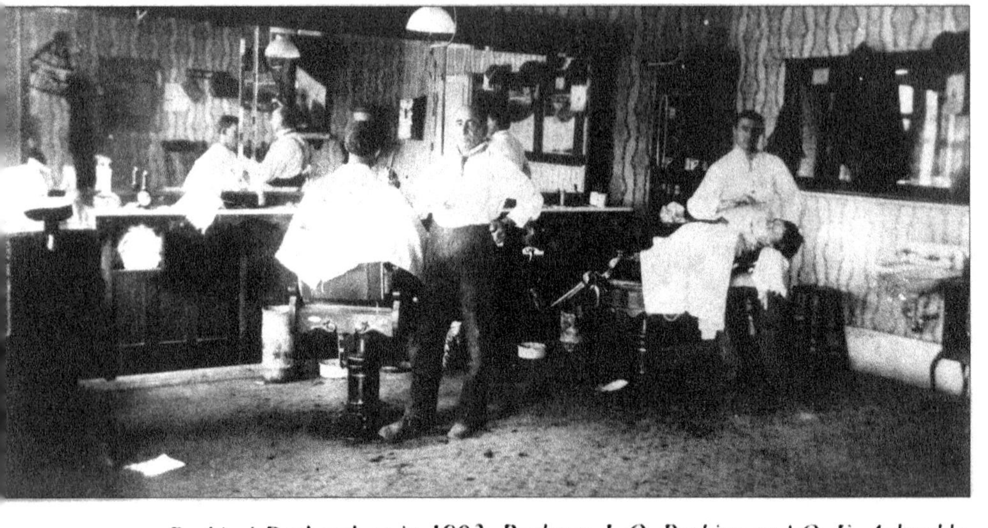

Perkins' Barbershop in 1903. Barbers: J. O. Perkins and O. E. Arbuckle.

Ray Barbershop about 1921. Barbers: Ponton, Roy Ray and D. B. Ray. Shop was first opened by Roy Ray in 1911.

A 1910 auto roundup, showing Elgin's first garage.

Big sale at Briscoe's Store, on Northside, in 1910.

VI UTILITIES

In Elgin's early days, individual wells and cisterns provided water, firewood and coal provided heat for comfort and cooking, and "coal oil" lamps and candles threw flickering circles of light for nighttime activities.

A public tank, at the present location of Davis and Schanhals Pontiac Co., provided water for many families and livestock in the vicinity. In times of drought, however, water supplies often proved inadequate—during one such shortage, the H & TC Railroad hauled in water, inviting all who were lacking to take what they needed from their cisterns.

Elgin's first municipal water system was built in 1892, consisting of a well and a short-lived water tower near the MK&T track. The elevated tank was of cypress, supported at a height of 30 or 40 feet by 8x8 timbers. Eliginites soon found that it was the strength of these timbers rather than the capacity of the tank, that determined how much water it could hold—one day it was overfilled and collapsed across the track.

The town then voted bonds for construction of a new water system, featuring five fire hydrants in the downtown section linked with cast iron pipe. This system also proved inadequate, ultimately failing entirely, and on September 12, 1901, an election was held to incorporate the City of Elgin for the purpose of securing a water supply of adequate capacity.

It was not until eight years later, however, that Elgin citizens finally could boast of a dependable water supply. During the period 1901-1908, citizen's groups met with repeated failure in their efforts to find a dependable source of water for the community. Finally, in December of 1908, an assemblage of Elgin citizens, meeting in the Woodmen of the World hall, voted issuance of $30,000 in bonds, and the project was again under way.

It was decided that Carr Springs, some five miles east of Elgin near the Balcones Fault, could supply enough water for the growing community's needs—in dry times of early days, it was a favorite camping ground for the indigenous Comanche Indians, as it was the only known water in a wide area. Later, stockmen drove whole herds there for water, and families would gather for community washing when home supplies dried up, the young ladies soaking their fine linen dresses in the iron oxide water until the desired golden brown shade was obtained.

The contract for the water plant was let to the J. W. Maxey Company of Houston, and on the morning of April 13, 1909, men and teams began clearing the ground around Carr Springs. The main line, replaced about 1917, was wire-wrapped wood pipe with wooden collars, laid in a ditch turned with an oversized road plow. On September 11, 1909, the water works was formerly turned over to the city—Elgin at last had water, and plenty of it.

Through the years, growth of the community of Elgin has been reflected in improvements to the water system—more fire hydrants, a 500 gallon-per-minute well at the city pump station, and in 1963, a new 500,000 gallon water tower visible for miles in the rolling countryside. In 1971, Elgin voters gave their approval to yet another bond issue for further sewer and water improvements.

When Elginites finally got running water into their homes, other "modern conveniences" were not far behind. At least two ice houses were in operation by 1909, and advertisements in the Elgin Courier touted John M. Puckett's acetylene gas machine and the Southern Light Company's gasoline lamps ("the safest, cleanest, and cheapest known") for home lighting.

In November, 1909, F. K. Leggett moved to Elgin from Livingston, Texas, and was granted a provisional franchise by the Board of Aldermen for an electric light plant, to be operated in conjunction with the ice factory he was building in the "Y" between the Central and Katy tracks. A month water, however, the city received another light proposal from Thomas L. Deisch of Helena, Arkansas. Mr. Leggett, acknowledging that he couldn't begin work on his electric plant until his icehouse was completed, withdrew his proposal, and Deisch and his brother Louie's Elgin Light and Power Company brought bright lights to Elgin in August of 1910. They bought out Leggett's ice factory, which he completed in April of 1910, later that same year. It was one of the most modern such facilities in the state at the time, with a capacity of nine to ten tons a day. Ice from the factory, delivered by wagon, sold for 40c per hundred pounds in hundred pound lots, or 50c per hundred when block cut.

The Elgin Power and Light Company was later sold to Mr. Zilker of Austin, who erected a new building to house it where the Ranch House Grocery and A. E. Johnson & Sons are now located on South Main Street. When Zilker sold the business in February of 1925, it changed hands three times in two years, going first to E. A. Clousnitzer of Kenedy, who sold out ten months later to the Texas Public Utilities Company. The Texas Power and Light Company bought the electric

A. M. Clopton and crew laying first water lines in 1909. John Culp home is on right.

First water lines were of wood, wire wrapped, with wooden collars.

properties from Texas Public Utilities and began serving the City of Elgin on December 6, 1926. TP&L moved into its new Elgin office in 1966. The all-electric office at 25 North Main Street, features an appliance repair service and a 40-person assembly room for civic gatherings.

The first decade of the twentieth century was a time of rapid technological change for Elgin—not only did the city get water and lights, but telephone service as well. In fact, Elgin had telephones before the water and light plants were even begun—Southwestern Bell records show telephone service established in Elgin in 1900—just 24 years after Alexander Graham Bell called out "Mr. Watson, come here, I need you."

Since history is nothing more than a story of events past, it is sometimes best told by a person who lived it; Miss Susie Taylor, who began work as a "local board girl" at $15 per month in 1903, had many recollections of those early days:

"As I remember it, the first Southwestern Bell Telephone board in Elgin was a small one, with space for 50 telephones. It was placed in Mrs. Lula Enders' Millinery Shop, and was tended by Mrs. Enders and her young assistant, Miss Nan Graham. It started with five telephones connected, as there was already a small local exchange here run by a Mr. St. Clair, connected with independant toll lines.

"At first, Southwestern had connections on toll—one line to Austin and one to Giddings. Later, the company moved to roomier quarters and put in a local board—we then had toll connections with Bastrop, Paige, and several smaller towns. This move brought more business phones as the Independent Company did not connect with Bastrop, the county seat.

"Miss Mary Scarborough took charge of Southwestern Bell work after the office was moved—to a brick building owned by W. H. Rivers on the south side of town. The lower floor was occupied by Jeff Meeks' dry goods and grocery store. Telephone service and installation was taken care of by a man who came out from Austin once or twice a week.

"Miss Scarborough handled the work by herself for a while, closing the switchboard about 9 o'clock at night. Later, I became night operator for the company.

"One night about midnight I had an urgent call—we'd had an awful sleet and freeze and everything was covered with ice. The outside stairway to the office had fallen down earlier in the day, leaving just the poles and a small landing on the outside standing, so we had to come up through another building and over an inside stairway. The party we were trying to reach had no telephone, and as we had no regular messenger service, we used young boys who had telephones in their homes—they were always happy to go for the fees. I instructed the boy how to get up into the offices when he came back with the messenger slip, but after an hour he had not arrived. I phoned his residence, but he had not returned. Finally he came in, skinned up and nearly frozen. When he handed me the signed messenger slip, I asked why he had been so long, as he had not had far to go. 'What do you think I am,' he replied. 'I climbed that pole four times and slipped back every time. I thought I never would get my feet on that landing.' He had climbed that outside pole covered with ice to the second story; a feat few linemen could perform with spurs on."

By 1908 the telephone company had grown to 200 subscribers and needed 16 toll or long distance lines to handle calls to and from Elgin. The Bell Company absorbed the Independent Company in 1925, adding 305 more subscribers and 15 toll lines to the local equipment. The company continued to grow with the community, and by 1948 there were 664 telephone subscribers in Elgin, with 46 waiting for service. At 1:01 a.m. Sunday, February 5, 1956, Elgin customers began to dail their own telephone calls. The new Elgin Dial Telephone Building was officially opened at 205 East Second Street at that time.

By 1970, a telephone company statistician reported that there were almost 2,000 telephones in the city, and that the average Elginite makes about 701 calls per year.

Looking back, there have been a lot of changes since the day when Miss Susie Taylor started her career as an operator. The magneto phone with the crank, the operator with her "Number, please," and the days when a long distance call was an unusual happening are all gone. Now communications satellites move across the atmosphere carrying calls from all over the world, television programs are carried over telephone cable and microwave, telephones in outdoor booths and even telephones in automobiles. In the future are picturephones and cordless telephones; data moving from one computer to the other at the rate of thousands of words per minute, and telephones that dial themselves when the called number is spoken aloud. It would seem ludicrous in 1900 if the people working in the first telephone exchange here had predicted these things. But—if it is true that the past is prologue—then perhaps those who look back in 50 years and read these words will not be surprised at all.

"When Elgin wants a thing done, her citizens just up and do it. Elgin has that kind of people," editorialized the Jubilee Edition of the *Elgin Courier* on May 21, 1936. The subject was natural gas, and as with the water works in earlier years, it was concerned Elgin citizens who had laid the groundwork for a necessary public utility.

A committee, composed of Charles J. Poth, Max Sandgarten, A. E. Johnson, Frank Swartz, and Louis Lundgren, had conferred with officials of the United Gas Company of Houston about bringing their service to Elgin, and were told that gas would be installed if 150 Elgin people would agree to subscribe to the service. The necessary subscribers were quickly found, and with considerable ceremony to properly

Inside the Deisch Brothers Light Plant in 1910.

Southwestern Bell Telephone Co. switchboard. Operators left to right: Estelle Casey, Irene Baker, Susie Taylor.

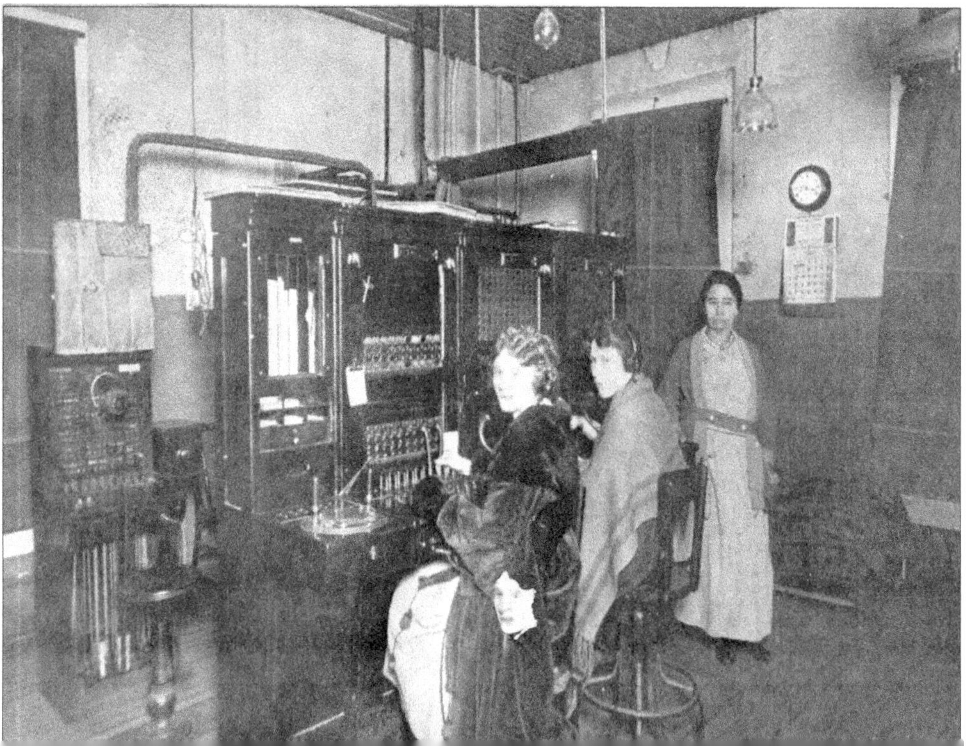

Eliza Carter, operator for Independent Telephone Co.

Switchboard at Southwestern Bell Telephone Co. on day that system was changed over to dial. Operators: Agnes Haverland, Ilex Carter, Lorene Prinz, Shirley Schmidt.

commemorate the event, a valve was turned on August 30, 1935 to permit natural gas to flow into the city's newly-completed distribution system. There were 185 initial customers.

United Gas opened its first office in Elgin in 1948, although, with the exception of the World War II period, a full-time representative had been located at Elgin since 1935. The company's new business office at 106 North Avenue C was opened on November 3, 1971.

As with other utilities, the gas company's growth has paralleled that of the community—at the end of 1971, United Gas had 1,289 customers in Elgin.

Committee responsible for bringing gas to Elgin in 1935. Front row; Max Sandgarten, Charles J. Poth. Back row: Frank Swartz, A. E. Johnson, Louis Lundgren.

VII ELGIN POST OFFICE 78621

Early in 1873 application was made to the Post Office Department for a post office to be established at Elgin. The Young's Settlement post office at Hogeye had been discontinued on December 8, 1872, when the postmaster, Dr. Samuel Sheasby, moved to Elgin to practice medicine. McDade served as the post office for Elgin for a brief time, with the mail being dropped off at the railroad depot.

On April 19, 1873, when the application was filled out, it was stated that the population to be served by the proposed office was 250. On May 13 of that year Edward Smithwick was appointed Elgin's first postmaster. He served only a few weeks, for on July 31 Richard V. Standifer was appointed to serve in his place. Standifer was also mayor of Elgin and operated the post office in his store at the corner of Main and Depot Streets. He sold this property to S. W. Biggs on March 3, 1877, and Biggs was appointed postmaster on July 2 that same year. A visitor to Elgin in 1886 described the post office at that time as "a little wooden shanty". A photograph prior to 1900 shows it located in a two-story frame building with a Grange store sharing the lower floor.

The post office was moved in 1904 to a brick building owned by Standifer's widow, Mrs. Texana Standifer, where the Eltex Theater stands today. Standifer, who died in 1889, erected the building in 1877 to house his general mercantile store. It was the first brick building in Elgin.

The third location of the post office was in the P. Bassist opera house building on the corner of Central and South Avenue C. It was located in the rear of the building, facing Avenue C. The opera house was built in 1906, and the post office was moved there in 1908.

An experiment by the Post Office Department, which they termed as "one of the most daring innovations of the twentieth century," was carried out in Elgin in the fall of 1912 when free mail delivery service was begun. In order to serve towns with populations under 5,000 this new system was approved and money appropriated by Congress. Fifteen towns in the United States were chosen, Elgin being the only town in Texas being named. An inspector came to Elgin and looked it over, stipulated a few requirements such as naming streets and numbering houses. Postmaster Burke, in cooperation with the City Council, set up all the requirements. On November 16, Joe Matthias became Elgin's first walking letter carrier. The entire state, as well as the nation, watched Elgin in this giant step the post office was making in expanding their services.

Records do not show exactly when the post office was moved to its fourth location, a building owned by Mrs. Florence Burke on Depot Street where the city water office is now located. It remained there until January 1, 1939, when it moved into the new federal building on North Avenue C.

In 1945, the old village delivery system was converted to city delivery, houses were again numbered, and streets named or renamed as most of the signs put up in 1912 had long disappeared. City delivery was extended to the new Sunset Heights addition in 1960.

In 1934, there were six Rural Free Delivery Routes out of the Elgin office, but due to better roads and better means of transportation, these have been combined into three routes.

On November 12, 1971, the Elgin post office was brought under the "Area Mail Processing Plan", and all outgoing mail is transported to the Austin Sectional Center for processing. The zip code for Elgin is 78621.

The postmasters from the beginning of the post office and the date of appointment are:

Edward Smithwick	May 13, 1873
Richard V. Standifer	July 31, 1873
S. W. Biggs	July 2, 1877
Demetrius Scott	November 20, 1877
Paul P. Woods	July 25, 1878
Julia K. Miles	December 12, 1883
Florence Sheasby	March 31, 1898
John L. Burke	May 15, 1908
J. W. Jackson	December 20, 1916
Florence B. Burke	January 25, 1922
Joseph H .King (acting)	August 1, 1925
Jesse C. Miller	April 15, 1926
Ernest N. Sowell	May 28, 1934
Paul G. Lundgren (acting)	October 4, 1960
Sadie B. Davis	September 30, 1963

Elgin's first post office.

Elgin's present post office.

VIII BUSINESS AND INDUSTRY IN ELGIN

Elgin's geographical location helped determine the impact business and industry would have on the town's growth. Deep beds of clay made Elgin the "Brick Capital of the Southwest." The rich, cotton-producing soil allowed many farmers to begin ginning operations which have continued a hundred years. Naturally, the banking and newspaper industries played important roles in Elgin's development. Also, the town's prominent position on railroad lines from all directions brought the flourishing of several hotels known well by Texas travelers in the early 1900's.

BRICK MAKING IN ELGIN

Brick manufacturing has been a major industry in Elgin since 1882. Deep beds of extra fine quality clay spread over several miles. As a result, Elgin has long been known as the "Brick Capital of the Southwest." Its first bricks were handmade, and later ones were manufactured "press" bricks.

Today, there are three highly mechanized brick plants producing a variety of bricks and ceramic tiles in 30 colors and three textures. The plants employ approximately 500 persons with an annual payroll of $2 million. More than 30 large trucks, most with self-loading and unloading equipment, handle the daily output of some 770,000 brick equivalent. They make deliveries throughout the United States and Mexico. In Mexico City alone, the U.S. Embassy, Governor's Palace and the National Airport are made of Elgin brick. The bricks are also shipped to Canada and Costa Rica.

Thomas O'Connor, an Irish-born brick contractor living in Austin, moved to Elgin in the late 1800's to build brick cisterns, wells and fireplaces, then in great demand in the growing community. He obtained his bricks from the Butler plant in Austin, but he soon discovered a fine bed of clay in his own area. In 1882, he began making bricks by hand, using wooden molds and at first drying them in the sun. A number of buildings built with handmade bricks are still in use in Elgin.

The Elgin Press Brick Company began operation in 1897, largely owned and managed by Morgan T. Smith who had come from the East. Bob Tinnen also seemed interested in the business. The company ceased manufacturing in 1912 when most of the supply of rich red clay inside the city east of the cemetery was exhausted.

The Lasher Brick Company, in business from 1906 to 1912, was located four miles south of Elgin on the present Bastrop Highway. It had much business until its main clay bed was used up. Today, the Acme Brick Company owns the land as a clay reserve.

In 1901, five miles east of town on present Highway 290, the Elgin Butler Brick Company opened as Elgin's third brick firm. It was founded by Michael (Mike) Butler, also a native of Ireland, who had built a brick factory in Austin after constructing one in St. Louis and one in Dallas. While many of his bricks were being shipped to Elgin, Butler became interested in the clay beds there and formed a company of local businessmen with himself as president. Today, members of the Butler family continue to operate the plant while residing in Austin. One of them commutes to Elgin, maintaining an office at the plant. The Butlers have a large manufacturing establishment and laboratory, and their engineers are constantly working on possibilities for new clay products.

Near the turn of the century, the Elgin Standard Brick Manufacturing Company was formed out of the Prewitt Brick Company. Owners of the latter, G. W., Ira A. and Dupree Prewitt of Elgin, formed a partnership with W. C. Rivers Sr., and W. H. Rivers Jr., also of Elgin, and joined in a corporation a short time later. The organization was begun in 1907 and completed in 1908 with a large plant on sizeable clay reserves. Wood, lignite, oil, electricity and now natural gas furnished the fuel for the plant. "Mr. George," G. W. Prewitt, resided with his family at the plant. He built and maintained some 70 brick and tile homes for many of his employees. He also kept an airplane and landing strip, golf course, fishing lake, bath house and landscaped grounds at the plant. In January of 1969, Elgin Standard merged with Elgin Butler.

Payne Brick Company, two miles south of Elgin on Highway 290, was founded by the six Payne brothers from Arkansas. These brick manufacturers made an exhaustive search throughout the South for good clay to use in a factory they planned to build, and Elgin was their choice. Laying of the foundation for the massive all-steel factory began in January of 1955. Their first brick run took place on December 1, 1956 from their continuous kiln and "U-shaped" drier, both 276 feet long. They installed the most modern brick manufacturing equipment and transformed 350,000 tons of mud a day into face bricks. The clay mixing and form machine produced 8,000 bricks per hour. Two

Thomas O'Conner home, built in 1890 from his own hand pressed brick.

Inside Elgin Press Brick Co. plant in 1906, where later Puckett's Gin stood near the H & T C Railroad.

Puckett's Ginnery, built in 1903, located east of M K & T Railroad. Mr. Puckett later owned a gin in the western part of town.

Hanke Gin soon after it was bought from John S. Smith in 1883. Was in continuous operation until 1970.

of the brothers now manage the plant and live in Elgin. The others are sales managers elsewhere, operating via a company airplane.

Modern offices are maintained at each of the three big plants at Elgin. Sales agency and other offices are kept in several cities.

ELGIN GINS

Elgin has had cotton gins since July 1878 when Madison Riggle sold 1½ acres to Silas Chatfield, who built a gin and grist mill where the present Hanke Gin stands. Chatfield sold the site on December 7, 1880 to John S. Smith, who had another person operate it.

On June 28, 1883, Smith sold his steam gin stand (80-saws) to Henry Hanke and to Hanke's cousin, John Frerich. Hanke had helped his contractor father, Franz Hanke, build log houses in Bastrop in 1854, and had often gone along to the Bastrop Arms Factory where his father repaired guns for the Confederate Army. Hanke later worked on ranches in Mason County and in West Texas. These experiences gave Hanke versatility which would be a benefit in later years.

Henry Hanke acquired full ownership of the gin in December, 1891. From then until 1969, the gin was run by Hanke and his sons, Frank and Fritz. They tore down and rebuilt the old gin in 1917 and converted the stand to diesel engine power. Frank outlived his brother and retired in 1969 at the age of 80, while retaining ownership of the property.

When the Hanke gin was purchased in 1883, it was a one-stand steam outfit, with a capacity of about 8 to 10 bales a day. Before it closed in 1969, it was a modern electric gin, capable of 4 to 5 bales per hour or about 50 to 60 bales a day. In earlier years, the cotton was carried from the farmer's wagon in baskets and was spread in the gin feeder by hand. The lint was blown into a large room and from there was carried by basket and put into the press. The power plant was a twenty-horsepower, two-flue boiler and an old steamboat engine that had seen service on the Mississippi River. The fuel was cord wood and cotton seeds, which in those days were of no value.

Before the Hanke Gin, farmers in nearby Perryville were serviced by different gins, including the Lawhon horse-drawn gin and the mule-powered Granville Tinnen gin and grist mill. Steam gins began in the mid-1870's in the area. Records show that R. S. (Bob) Tinnen had a horse-drawn gin on River Road two and a half miles south of Elgin in the mid-1870's but he sold his steam engine, hydraulic press, suction fan, pulleys, shafts and gin house for $1,000 to L. L. (Lynn) Puckett on January 1, 1894. Puckett erected a gin on Lot 3 of Miles Addition in Elgin near the present site of the grain and feed elevator. The four Puckett brothers jointly owned the gin for some time, but finally full ownership went to T. J. Puckett. He had had the earlier experience of operating his father's horse-drawn gin.

Puckett sold the gin to American Round Bale Company on May 16,

Inside the Elgin National Bank on the Southside. W. H. Rivers, Sr., Bank President, is standing in center.

View of Southside Elgin in 1908, showing the Elgin National Bank on the corner of South Main and Central Avenue. The A. J. Miller laundry wagon, to the right, is driven by Adolph Sowell.

1900. The gin had round and square bale facilities. American Round Bale Company then leased the operation to Anderson-Clayton Cotton Company of Houston. Under the lease the gin's management passed from W. S. Martin to Chester Owens to C. D Hays. During Martin's operation, his daughter, Sadie (later Mrs. W. E. McCullough) was the first woman cotton buyer in Texas. She helped in her father's gin program, having studied cotton classing in the Anderson-Clayton office in Houston.

By 1925, T. J. Puckett again owned the steam gin and converted it to electric power. He then sold it in 1929 to R. A. Hiller, who sold the gin in 1968 to Leroy Weiss and son, Lamar Weiss, of Manor, the present owners.

In 1903, T. J. Puckett built a new square-bale saw-gin. He sold his nearby round bale operation in 1909 to Farmers Gin Company. The company's officers included C. F. Berg, president, Martin Ahlquist, John Victor Morrell and John Rolf. They later sold the gin to other businessmen.

Puckett also bought the Deener Drug Store, but three years later returned to his ginning. In 1912, he built a new steam gin at the site of the old Elgin Press Brick Co. But the gin burned in 1924, and Puckett built a new brick building there in 1925 with deisel engines as a power source. Use of the new gin was discontinued in 1957.

Elgin also had the Dorris Gin which stood where the present Swenson Gulf Consignee Office stands and there were possibly two other gins at different locations. On August 11, 1896, J. F. (Bob) Dorris sold one gin stand, grist mill, boiler and engine to G. H. Cassel who moved it to his two-acres near Ramsey School east of Elgin. Later the Little Elf Filling Station stood at the site.

At Pleasant Grove, just east of Elgin, Pressley George also operated a horse-drawn gin on land he bought in 1865. The gin burned in 1894. Jack Gillum reported that he saw the fire miles away from his father's farm located on the present old McDade Road.

Williams Owens built a steam-powered gin and grist mill at Pleasant Grove in 1882. One of the Stone brothers, who then lived near the mill, noted that it burned in 1914.

Only the Weiss gin is still in operation in Elgin.

ELGIN BANKS

The Elgin National Bank, formerly the Bank of Elgin, has had a strong tradition in the Elgin area. The Bank of Elgin was begun in 1891 and was privately owned by W. H. (Bud) Rivers, an early merchant, landowner and businessman. Rivers was the son of Rev. Wm. I. Rivers, a Methodist circuit rider and former chaplain in the Confederate Army.

The Bank of Elgin was located in part of the large Rivers and Carter brick store on South Side. The building was built as the Rivers and Gresham Store in 1881, but eight years later it became the Rivers and

In 1923 the Elgin National Bank moved to its present location on the southeast corner of North Main and First Streets.

Street scene showing the Merchants and Farmers State Bank in background which was organized in 1906.

Inside of Merchants and Farmers State Bank.

Merchants and Farmers State Bank moved to a new location on the southwest corner of Main and First Streets. Building was erected in 1911.

Inside view of the ELGIN COURIER *plant in 1898 when it was owned by S. J. Isaacks and C. W. Webb. From left to right: S. J. Isaacks, C. W. Webb, and Bazil Olds.*

Built in 1910 by J. O. Smith, this building housed the ELGIN COURIER *and commercial plant for over forty years. Recently remodeled, it is now the home of Weed Instrument Company.*

Carter Store. Rivers and A. H. Carter were co-owners, the latter selling his interest to W. H. Carter, brother-in-law of Rivers. In 1905, the store became the Rivers Brothers Mercantile Company. Rivers owned most of the company, the remaining interests going to two of his sons, M. L. (Leon) and W. C. (Wayland) Rivers.

On April 21, 1906, the Bank of Elgin was incorporated at its same location as the Elgin National Bank with a capital stock of $50,000, with W. H. Rivers as its president. James Keeble was cashier and W. H. Rivers, Jr., was assistant cashier.

In September 1923, the bank moved from South Side to its present, more modern Main Street building on North Side, opposite the Merchants and Farmers State Bank. Several improvements have been made since its relocation, including the new glassed-in front lobby, a night depository, drive-in facilities and a large rear parking area for personnel and customers.

W. H. Rivers, the bank's founder, died in the summer of 1909. Since its beginning in 1891, the bank has been operated by members of the Rivers family, except for two brief periods. In 1901, a short time elapsed between the founder's death and the election of his widow as president. In March of 1960, R. H. Arbuckle Sr. was president, following the death of W. H. Rivers Jr., until W. H. Rivers III was elected in January 1961 as president of the bank. Following his death in 1971, Lawson Rivers, another grandson of the founder, became president.

In 1956, the Elgin National Bank had assets of $3,500,000, the largest of any bank in Bastrop County. In December 1969, its deposits were $7,247,666.42. Assets further increased from October 1970, totaling $7,827,993.81, to December 1971, with a total of $8,412,000.

Elgin had a second bank, the Merchants and Farmers State Bank, on Main Street, organized on December 16, 1906. It was first located in the building north of the present Upchurch Drug Store, but it was later moved to the northwest corner of a roomy two-story red brick building on Main Street, opposite the present Elgin National Bank. In 1908, the *Elgin Courier* noted that the bank had added to its prestige by enhancing its appearance with new fixtures.

Otto Bengtson was the bank's first president, C. F. Berg was first vice president, A. F. Anderson was second vice president, and Carl Carlson was cashier. The directors were J. Victor Morell, A. J. Anderson and John O. Sponberg. The Merchants and Farmers State Bank later became the Elgin State Bank, but all services were discontinued in 1939.

NEWSPAPERS IN ELGIN'S HISTORY

Weekly newspaper publishing was one of the early businesses in Elgin's formative years. The Elgin *Meteor* was the first journalistic venture, publishing papers in 1879 and 1880. The Elgin *Times* was established in 1882 and was edited by C. D. Green for several years. It then was sold to C. S. Seay and subsequently sold to Ebb B. Hurt the following year. Hurt, a lawyer, was the son of Judge R. E. Hurt and son-in-law of Governor John Ireland. He came to Elgin in 1890 to practice law and published his weeklies in a plant at his home. The site was located where the Assembly of God Church now stands.

Hurt was already publisher of the Elgin *Leader* when he acquired the *Times*. The *Leader* passed to an unknown publisher, but in 1901 it was being published by Ben L. Grimes. George C. Staples joined Grimes as a partner for a year, then sold his interest back to Grimes, who in turn sold to Dr. W. C. Smith, owner of the *Elgin Courier*. In 1907 the *Texas Bladet,* a Swedish paper, was established and was published in the *Courier* plant until 1908 when it was moved to Austin.

The *Courier* was established March 21, 1890, by Miles H. Hill, a local lawyer, who was its publisher for approximately a year. At the time, George R. Allen also was associated with the paper.

J. O. Smith, son of Dr. W. C. Smith, later wrote in his "reminiscings" that the first location of the *Courier* was a wooden shanty back of O'Connor Furniture Store.

A year after its establishment, the *Courier* was purchased by S. T. (Tom) Cain and was moved upstairs over O'Connor's store. It was published at this location for several years. On September 1, 1897, Cain retired from the field of publishing and became an agent for Waters Pierce Oil Company. After ten years with this company, Cain opened a drug store in Elgin which he operated until his death in 1943.

Taking over the *Courier* in 1897 from Cain were S. J. Isaacks and C. W. Webb, who later were lawyers in Elgin. Judge Webb sold his half interest to his partner after one year of publishing. At the time, the plant was on the second floor of the old red brick Masonic building, where the Elgin National Bank's drive-through facilities now are found. Equipment at the plant consisted of a Washington hand press, a small job press and several cases of hand-set type. Judge Isaacks later bought a new press, another job press and a better assortment of type. He operated the paper until 1901. In 1903, he served his first term in the Texas House of Representatives from Bastrop County. After moving from Elgin to West Texas, he served as a representative from El Paso from 1938 to 1945. He died in 1956. Judge Webb continued to practice law in Elgin until his death.

In November of 1901, J. O. Smith with his father, Dr. W. C. Smith, purchased the *Courier*. The son became sole owner shortly thereafter, because of his father's failing health. Dr. W. C. Smith died in 1908. J. O. Smith continued building the newspaper he was to operate for over 46 years. During the early 1900's the *Courier* grew from a small operation into one of the most modern and well equipped plants found in any small town in Texas. As Elgin grew, the *Courier* also grew. It added modern equipment and expanded its personnel and staff to produce a quality printed weekly paper and job work.

Inside view of the plant of the **ELGIN COURIER** *soon after it moved into its new building on Depot Street in 1910. J. O. Smith, owner and publisher of the weekly paper, stands beside a hand-fed job press (right); Pat Burns in the center and Bill Billingsley (far left) stands atop the Cranston cylinder press which turned out the* **COURIER** *for over forty years. A gasoline motor in the left foreground powered the machinery by a shaft and pulleys coming from the ceiling.*

Mr. and Mrs. J. O. Smith stand outside the Courier building when they retired from publishing the paper in 1947. Mr. Smith purchased the weekly in 1901 and with the help of Mrs. Smith operated it for over 46 years.

Older volumes of the *Courier* are now priceless editions of historical information. Names, births, deaths, business establishment information, socials, entertainment, city politics, progress of the town etc. all blend into a preservation of the past. For example, in 1926 editor J. O. Smith reflected in his "reminiscings" on the 25 years he had been in Elgin. He wrote of his arrival in 1901 to buy the *Courier:*

"C. W. Webb, a promising young attorney, drew up the papers. His office was over Jeff Meeks' store, where Sam Culp's Hardware Store (southside) is now located. The plant consisted of a Vaughn Ideal hand press, an 8x12 job press and a handfull of type in the front upstairs room of the Masonic building now occupied by the Independent Telephone Co. (more recently by the bank drive-in).

"When we arrived, we got off the Katy train at a small dilapidated frame passenger depot. In front of the depot was a stock pen for loading cattle. That was where the McClellan Inn now is located. There was also a cotton patch where the oil mill now stands.

"We spent the night in the old brick hotel then operated by a Mr. Joiner. An old brick building stood on the corner where the old Elgin National Bank building (southside) now stands. Then it was occupied by W. H. Carter and Company, general merchandise. Back where McCreery's Garage stands today was a 'public tank' where everybody got water, including cattle, hogs, etc.

"W. H. Rivers owned the Bank of Elgin located next to W. H. Carter and Company. John Parnell had a barber shop in a little frame building where the Bassist Opera House is now. Thomas O'Connor's furniture store was the only building on that block, except for the building now occupied by Hardwick news stand.

"Where the present Elgin National Bank building stands, Uncle Larry Scarbrough had a blacksmith shop. Residences were found on both sides of the street in the next block. The Puckett addition then was a cotton patch. The Tingle addition, where the new high school is being built, was way out in the country."

In July 1910, J. O. Smith mentioned the several locations of the *Courier* since its establishment, while inviting his readers to visit him in his new building on Depot Street (now Weed Instrument). He explained that the growth of the business necessitated a move from the Masonic building to another location across the street, presently the location of Jones Drug Store. Later another move was made into a building built by Judge Gillespie, next door to Mutual Lumber Co. It then was located where city park lies, between Depot Street and the railroad. Smith wrote that Judge Gillespie had to add another 50 feet to the existing 50-foot building because so much new machinery—linotype machine, paper cutter, perforator, stapler, power presses, etc.—had been jammed into the space. They moved the paper into a new building erected for the expressed purpose of housing the *Courier* without missing an issue of the paper. "It was a lot of work, but we are the proud possessor of a nice, new and modern building of our own," Smith wrote. He also elaborated on the changes of modern equipment, saying the days of "sticking" (hand-setting) type was past.

In 1908 he purchased a linotype machine. In that day, it was a "newfangled" machine that set type by molding lines from metal rather than hand picking each letter from a case of type. Another linotype, a Model 19, was installed in 1917 and was used until the paper changed to offset printing in 1957. This machine is still in operation in another part of the state. Smith pointed out that the move in 1910 put the *Courier* plant less than one hundred feet from its original site. When electricity came to Elgin earlier in 1910, the *Courier* was hooked up with electric motors, replacing the gasoline motor as its power source.

In 1924 Smith purchased the Bastrop *Advertiser*, which he published until 1930 when his son-in-law and daughter, Mr. and Mrs. R. E. Standifer became the publishers. The *Advertiser* is still owned and published by the Standifers and their son, Bob.

J. O. Smith was an Elgin booster, giving liberally his time and newspaper space to promote worthwhile projects for the town. He saw Elgin grow from a population of 1258 in 1901 to 3,500 at his retirement. Highly civic minded, he fostered many suggestions for improvement. He pointed out in his weekly editorials the advantages that Elgin could offer industrial and business ventures. As city councilman and editor in 1909, he helped bring water to Elgin. He also encouraged the organizing of a fire department and was in influence in the securing of Elgin's city park, high school, post office, hospital and Elgin Memorial Park. He organized Elgin's Chamber of Commerce, serving several terms as its president. Smith also served in the Kiwanis Club, among other organizations. He was the first person to be named "Most Worthy Citizen" in Elgin.

Though not a lawyer, Smith was a politician of renown and served his district for seven terms in the House of Representatives. First elected in 1916, Smith held terms during both world wars.

In all Smith's accomplishments, the inspiration and assistance of his wife, "Miss Daisy," played a large role. Despite widespread interests and activities—including clubs, church and music—Mrs. Smith found time to take over management of the *Courier* when legislative duties demanded her husband's time and later when his health failed. She was active in the publishing of the *Courier* to the last day of their ownership of the paper, serving as advertising director and looking after the front office. The Smiths moved to Bastrop in 1948 to be near their children. J. O. Smith died on December 27, 1959 at the age of 87.

Many young men learned the printer's trade in Smith's plant. Some established papers of their own elsewhere. Others joined the dailies in some of Texas' larger cities. Still others devoted their time to the commercial printing field.

Two employees, Pat Burns and Mrs. Lena Finch, gave many years in service to the *Courier*. Burns went to work for Smith soon after arriving in Elgin, becoming plant foreman and later city editor. Mrs. Finch was reporter, writer and gracious front office lady for the *Courier* for almost 40 years.

On January 1, 1948, the masthead of the *Courier* bore the name of a new owner and publisher for the first time in 46 years. Don Scarbrough, then of Taylor, purchased the plant and building from Smith and published the *Courier* for two years. Scarbrough, who owned several other weekly papers in neighboring towns, sold to W. Gregory Hale in 1950. Hale published the paper for only four months before selling to C. A. and Bonner McMillion from Falls County.

The McMillions published the paper from November 6, 1950 until May of 1952 when they sold it to Edwin Bronaugh. Bronaugh had owned and operated a daily at Commerce. On December 21, 1954, Bronaugh died after a few months of poor health. He was the first *Courier* editor to die while owning the paper. Mrs. Bronaugh continued to publish the paper until June of 1956 when she sold it to Harold H. Bredlow.

Bredlow and his son, Robert, then managing editor, remodeled the building, bought new equipment and in 1957 changed the method of printing from hot metal and cylinder press to cold type and offset printing. This step brought the *Courier* abreast of innovations in the printing industry. Along with several co-publishers and associates, Bredlow published the paper until the present management took over in 1964. In that period Sam Braswell was publisher during part of 1961-62. William Smith followed as publisher for approximately a year.

On July 1, 1964, a group of young men from Austin and San Marcos bought the *Courier*. The present owner, Bob Barton, was part of that group but later sold to Orville Mosher. Mosher managed the *Courier* for 18 months and tried to start another paper, The Elgin *News*. That venture failed. As a result the *Courier* was again taken up in early 1967 by Barton, the present publisher of the 82-year-old weekly paper that has seen much of Elgin's history in the making.

HOTELS

The first hotel built in Elgin was the Joplin Hotel of plank construction located on Main Street. An old Negro man, "Uncle Tom Goody," drummed for the Joplin, meeting the trains and singing his song:

"Calhoun's Saloon and Standifer's Street.
Joplin's Hotel and nothing to eat."

Townsfolk of the day danced to Uncle Tom Goody's fiddle.

In 1876, Mrs. Sallie McDonald traded a small farm for a hotel in Elgin while her husband ran a livery barn. Business was good for Mrs. McDonald.

Elgin's City Hotel, located on Depot Street in the 1890s.

A reunion of veterans in front of the City Hotel in 1895. Some of those pictured are: Jacob Standifer, veteran of the Texas Revolution; F. S. Wade; William Owens; W. H. Rivers; Bob Jones; Jim Litton; Joe Bennett; John Chiles; Judge Gillespie; Messrs. Quin, Pfeiffer, Martin, McDonald.

Old red brick hotel built in 1897, located south of the H & T C Railroad facing the Union Depot. Later became Johnson's Nursing Home.

McClellan Inn built in 1908. Located near the intersection of the H & T C and M K & T Railroads, east of Union Depot.

The City Hotel, also known as Meeks Hotel, was owned in the mid-1890's by Frank Meeks. Located halfway down Depot Avenue facing the railroad, the hotel burned on October 2, 1898.

In 1897 a large two-story red brick structure, the Elgin Hotel, was built on the south side of the H & T C Railroad. Operated for many years by the Wilkes family, the Elgin Hotel had a spacious basement, dining room and kitchen with full length bannistered porches across the front of the building. Only a few steps from the Union Passenger Depot of the M K & T and H & T C Railroads, the hotel flourished. The Elgin Hotel was known for its hospitality and attracted passengers day and night off trains from all directions. It later became a nursing home, first operated by Mr. and Mrs. Milton Johnson. The building was torn down in 1963.

McClellan Inn, built in 1908 across from the Union Depot, was located near the intersection of the H & T C and M K & T Railroads. It was constructed of timbers from the huge pleasure craft "Ben Hur," which plied the waters of the Colorado River in the 1890's, affording the elite of Austin and Central Texas the tops in entertainment. When this famous boat was taken out of service, Mr. Tom Pfeiffer of Elgin purchased and dismantled it, using the lumber in the building of McClellan Inn.

The inn had 22 bedrooms, a dining room, kitchen and office, all of which were very spacious. Its attic was the size of six or eight more rooms or a large dance hall. The building was lighted throughout with acetylene.

After it was finished, the hotel was leased to Miss Ethel McClellan, then proprietress of the "Millet Mansion" in Austin. Miss McClellan was known by the traveling public as one of the best hotelwomen in Texas, and the McClellan Inn became a hostelry that traveling men "made" every week to enjoy the gracious atmosphere and unexcelled cuisine.

In 1910 a new time card was issued by the H & T C Railroad which scheduled the 1:37 train to reach Elgin at 12:15. The train stopped twenty minutes for dinner, and Miss McClellan was in charge of feeding the passengers.

After she died in 1926, her husband, John Flowers, continued operating the McClellan Inn until failing health forced his retirement. The famous hotel later was owned by several others. Shortly after 6 o'clock on the morning of October 23, 1952, flames roared high, demolishing the historic Elgin inn. That blaze ended 44 years of hospitality and fine foods for the Texas traveling public.

Elgin Oil Mill, organized in 1906, with Charles Berg serving as manager. Picture taken in 1908. Later E. O. Lundgren, Sr. became owner-manager of the business.

IX EDUCATION

Getting a family settled and building a new home on undeveloped land demands much thought, planning, and expenditure of energy, whether in 1872 or in 1972. Thus, the first two years of Elgin's growth were busy ones for the group of people lured to the area by the railroad, the good natural resources, and the mild climate. Although the Burleson Branch log school on the Pressley E. George farm remained in operation less than two miles east of the community, on the present Farm to Market Road 3000, many early-comers felt that establishing a permanent home temporarily took precedence over their children's educational needs.

The first school bell to ring in Elgin was heard in 1874, when A. H. Carter of Alabama, after two terms at the Burleson Branch School, began classes for 172 scholastics in a building located at the present site of West Third between Avenue A and Avenue B. To care for this large enrollment Mrs. C. W. Brooks and Mrs. Will Jones were employed as assistants. The school was supported by subscriptions and tuition—the usual tuition fee being one or two dollars per child per month. This school building on West Third Street, with the addition made by the Masonic Lodge in 1881, continued to serve the educational needs of the community until the growth in scholastics caused the lodge to move to another location in November 1897.

Since the early education of Elgin's children was entirely dependent on private schools, ministers or others with some educational background often would open classes in their homes for instruction in the basics. S. B. Whipple and his wife, Mary, held such classes in their two-story home at the present 24-28 North Main.

In the *Bastrop Advertiser,* September 13, 1879, William A. Bowen announced for September 22, 1879, the first session of the Elgin High School, a private institution "with the lowest terms, in keeping with the stringent times." He added that "a thorough knowledge of the subject matter will be necessary for a broad and full mental culture."

Elgin citizens, anxious for the early development of their children's education, enrolled them in different private schools before they were of school age. Jack Gillum in 1894 attended a one room school taught by Mrs. M. B. Keeble in a classroom in the backyard of her home at the corner of Avenue A and Central Avenue. Professor Bolle conducted a German School for two summers and was succeeded by a Miss Kessel of Bastrop. Frank Hanke numbered among the children of German parentage in attendance. At the beginning of the new century Joe Haynie learned his ABC's from Mrs. Gray whose school was across from the South School.

The private school continued to be the chief means of education, until the Texas school law implemented the community school system. This system allowed parents to organize into free school communities, to share in the benefits of the available school fund, to yearly petition the county judge for permission to organize free public schools and to appoint three trustees.

By 1890, there were 95 such community schools operating in the county. Elgin, with its 151 students, ranked fourth in scholastics. The next year, Elgin Community School had the largest enrollment in the county, with 188 pupils. The judge appointed A. H. Carter, Gus H. Jones, and J. W. Standifer as school trustees to serve both years. The appropriation of $981 was an increase of $196 over the previous year.

An early community school was conducted by Principal H. W. Stevens for 91 pupils in 1891. Misses Hattie Stevens, Bettie Dew, and Jewel McCullough served as assistant teachers. To supplement the available school fund, each child of scholastic age paid a $1.00 tuition fee, while over age students paid more.

Within a few years a group of interested citizens, led by W. H. Rivers, Dr. G. T. King, and *Elgin Courier* editor S. T. Cain, realized that organizing the school program with new trustees each year left much to be desired and began advocating that the town of Elgin be incorporated for more permanence in school planning. As a result, Elginites on June 18, 1897, voted 137-32 to incorporate the Elgin Independent School District, and to levy tax of 50 cents on the hundred dollar valuation on property owners for the erection of a suitable school building. The district's first trustees were W. H. Rivers, Gust Rehfeld, Walter Keeble, J. C. Chiles, and M. T. Smith.

September 5, 1898, the opening date of the newly completed eight-room, two-story red brick schoolhouse, still standing on South Avenue C, found two-hundred pupils enrolled under Principal J. M. Hale, who also taught grades seven through ten, while Misses Goldsmith and Maude Campbell and Mrs. McMullen taught the first six grades.

First graduates of the new Elgin school were Bennie Glasscock and Misses Georgia Fisher and Nannie Smith, who completed their studies in 1900. With the exception of 1910, when the eleventh grade was added, Elgin High School has graduated seniors each year since. In

1913, the smallest senior class on record was composed of Misses Nell Owens and Grace Lanfear. The largest class of this early period, the class of 1909, graduated eighteen. By 1918, one hundred forty-four students claimed Elgin High as their Alma Mater.

As well as the first graduating class, 1900 marked other educational advances for Elgin. A county teacher's institute was held February 23-24 at Elgin, and a county "normal" school, for preparation of teachers, was organized. Teachers' institutes were a part of the on-going training of educators at that time, providing a place to discuss common school problems with other teachers, to plan a uniform course of study, and to "relate socially and professionally with other teachers in the county and the community in general." A program for the 1900 institute lists such topics by Elginites as "The Cooperation of Parents", by Judge C. W. Webb: "Some Changes Since We Were Boys" by W. H. Rivers and S. J. Isaacks; and presentations by two teachers, Misses Stubbs and Goldstein, on "Do our teachers of language teach the pupils to use their mother tongue correctly? If not, why?", and "The importance of good reading for pupils", respectively. The closing number on the program was a general discussion on "the teacher who has spasms."

It was a discussion at this institute that brought about the opening of a Bastrop County Normal School at Elgin on June 4, 1900. The six-week school, designed to equip elementary and high school graduates certification at their respective levels, incorporated both pre-service and in-service training and attracted would-be teachers from many nearby counties, and from as far away as Mississippi and Virginia. The faculty included superintendents from Bastrop, San Marcos, and Austin, as well as Mrs. P. T. Miller and Mrs. E. H. Jenkins of Bastrop. Mr. J. H. Gilaspy, W. I. Rowe, and Mrs. E. H. Jenkins served on the county board of examiners.

In the century's first decade of technological progress, interest in scientific training grew, but suitable laboratory equipment for the school could not be provided from the available school fund. Local talent met the challenge in 1905 with one of the first of many school benefits. "The Deestrick Skule," with J. C. Schermerhorn as teacher and L. H. Scarborough as "the baby brother", was staged that year in the Falls Building, which was "taxed to the uttermost to hold the crowd, and many being unable to get in left."

By 1909, the red brick South School, which had seemed so spacious in 1898, was badly overcrowded. The library had been divided into two extra classrooms, and children were attending on a half-day schedule. Elgin citizens, realizing that expansion was the only answer, voted a $10,000 bond issue to erect a new building facing Avenue H on a lot purchased from A. H. Carter in northeast Elgin between Beaukiss Lane and East 6th.

A contract was let to J. W. Rucker of Elgin for $7,947.00 on March 30, 1910. The Mutual Lumber Company was to furnish the material. The school board members, J. C. Miller, president; P. Bassist, vice-president; W. H. Rivers, secretary; J. S. Sharp, J. T. Lawhon, Otto Bengtson, and R. S. Deener, invited State Superintendent of Public Schools F. M. Bralley to deliver the address when the marble corner stone was laid by the Elgin Masonic Lodge June 3, 1910. This cream colored brick building, called the North School, opened September 1910 with Buckner Harris serving as superintendent. This new North School provided classes for grades one through seven; Miss Clara Stubbs was the principal of this elementary school; Misses Kate Christian, Fay Bunker, and Adella Kesselus, assistants. The high school faculty, with Miss Kate Gannaway as principal, consisted of Misses Amelia Nelson and Winnie McCall. The South School elementary teachers were: Misses Lucy Blocker, Jennie Wolliver, Salita Darden, America Judkins, and Evelyn Gillespie.

By 1917, twenty years after the system's foundation, the four-square-mile Elgin school system was meeting the educational needs of 444 white, 222 Negro, and 35 Mexican students. In addition to the two eight-room brick school buildings, the district supported a one-room frame school for Mexican students, a three-room Negro school, "a splendid library valued at about $500", and two modern science laboratories. Among the 16½ affiliated units were Latin, German, trigonometry, two credits in science, and Domestic Economy to be added the following year.

World War I was on, and Elgin students responded patriotically with thrift stamp buying campaigns, organized by class into war saving societies—Matthis' War Saving Society, John Nichols' Rootes Rooting Society, and Democracy War Saving Society—who bought a Liberty Loan Bond. They helped the Red Cross, cultivated a war garden, and raised a service flag bearing the names of all ex-students in the armed forces. Ollie Pfeiffer, a senior, enlisted in the Army.

By 1921, a new building, consisting of two class rooms and a utility room, had been erected on Williams Street for the Mexican students. This school remained in operation until 1947 when the Elgin School Board arranged to have all Mexican children attend the Elgin Public Schools.

Elginites again faced the problem of inadequate school facilities in their growing community by 1925. The high school lacked sanitary facilities and laboratory space was insufficient. Following a meeting on December 14, 1925, with the Retail Merchants' Association and the Parent Teacher Association, the school board called for a $94,000 bond issue election for a new high school. Despite drouth years which threatened Elgin's agricultural economy, the bond issue carried, and classes were held for the first time in the new High School building on North Avenue C on February 3, 1927. The building, with additions and barracks, is still in use today.

The Elgin Independent School District has progressed with its community since that time, with citizens voting bonds as needed for expansion. A new elementary school on West Second Street opened in 1954, and Elgin Junior High School was completed ten years later also on West Second.

In 1965, Elgin schools were integrated under the freedom of choice plan, bringing to a close a long history of "separate but equal" education going back to 1882, when Professor Robert Robertson schooled 25 Negro pupils in "the three R's" at the site of Westbrook Cemetery. Churches were the center for early-day Negro education, and in 1891 the newly-formed "Little Flock" Baptist Church founded another school to supplement that at the cemetery. Teachers' salaries were low, school terms short, and discipline was the earmark of a good school Many pupils dropped out at an early age to help their parents with farming chores. Early teachers included Professor Wash Chambers of Sayersville, Mrs. Ada Connally of Austin, Mrs. Mattie Gregg, Mrs. W. H. Shelborn of Oberlin, Ohio, Albert Waltrous of Austin, Mrs. Victoria Bailey of Winchester, Mrs. Virginia McFaul of Bastrop, a Mr. Glass and a Mrs. Juanita Lee of Cedar Creek, and J. W. Patton of Alexander, Alabama. Patton later married Miss Lula Belle Westbrook, and both taught in the community's Negro schools until 1914.

Growth of Negro educational facilities continued after being absorbed by the Elgin School District. J. C. Madison succeeded J. W. Patton as principal of the Negro school in 1914, and served until 1940, when D. P. Johnson was selected as principal of the Washington School. In 1925, the old Washington School, a white frame building, had been erected to take care of the increase in scholastics; and in 1960, a brown brick building, which included a gymnasium-auditorium combination, was built on South Avenue F. When the school system was totally integrated the latter building became the Junior High School for the system.

The school district has expanded in area from the original four square miles to one hundred sixty-eight square miles with six school buses conveying those students who live outside the two-mile limit in the consolidated system.

The scholastic population, which was 418 students in 1913-14, with no school for Mexican students and an average daily attendance of 73% for the whites and 33% for the Negroes, increased until in 1938-39 there were 871 students with an average daily attendance of 92%. To keep abreast of the population increase, the school budget has increased as well as the total evaluation of property.

1936-37—Total value of buildings and equipment approximately $200,000.00 with 21 employees

1958-59—the budget was set for $317,358.00 with 1,197 students

1964-65—1,348 scholastics, with an average daily attendance of 929.17 for white and 451.72 for Negroes, with a budget set for $470,110.00

1971-72—1,572 students with a budget of $900,175.00 and value of property and equipment $1,500,000.00.

Elgin school system had been making provision for special education for some years, but in 1971-72 the system was selected to be one of the forerunners in the State's Plan A Special Education. This enables the system to offer services in the following areas: Educational Mental Retarded, Trainable Mental Retarded, Early Childhood Education, Language and/or Learning Disabled, and Vocational Training for the retarded learner.

The aim of the Elgin High School has always been to graduate students who could be able to relate theory with reality and education with living. Thus she looks with pride when her graduates return to the community to become a part of it. Her late mayor, Franklin Condron, and present mayor, W. E. Arbuckle, Jr. are El-Hi graduates. Her graduates are numbered among the City Council and are serving on the board of trustees for the system that graduated them. The Elgin Independent School District in 1971-72 had the following graduates employed: Raymond Johnson, building custodian; Alice Lynn Jarmon Brandt, Mary Gregg Hendricks Christensen, Joy Cole Fromme, Dorothy Butler Huff, Margy R. Davenport Danklefs, and Jane Whitehead Wiley, teachers' aides; Primary teachers, Velma Leseman, Maurine Harris Nairn, Ruth Lauman Schanhals, and Jane Rivers; Elementary teachers, Eleanor Ruth Carter Frost, Esther Swenson Gustafson, and Paul Wayne Walker; High School teachers, Camilla Oden Talbot, Thelma Fitzpatrick Harrison, Gene McVay, Milton Dusek, and Bobby Joe McClendon; business office personnel, Becky Huff Huggins, Beth Barrington Staton, and Bob McClendon. Edward Brandt, 1945 graduate, principal of Junior High School, is the first male to become a principal. Previously two women, Kate Christian Gillum, 1903, and Modene Griffin, 1918, served as principals of the South School. Fontaine R. Mathis, 1905, was the only graduate to date who served as superintendent of schools.

As scholastics have been important to Elgin schools through the years, so have other activities been designed to recognize the complete needs of children in the system. The organization of a student council in 1913 offered Elgin's high school students a part in student government, and was instrumental in the beginning of the honor system, "to put before the students some tangible ideal by which they may be guided." Members of that first council included Susie Taylor, president, Mattie Mae Carter, secretary, and class representatives Don Gillum, Amy Walling, Marvin Standifer, Lillian Martinson, James Moore, Marjorie Meeks, Carroll Kimball, Modene Griffin, and Alton Davis.

Other early school organizations included the Sydney Lanier Society, which offered training in parliamentary procedure and student participation and was the forerunner of many of today's departmental clubs, and the Future Teachers, organized in 1916 by Lucille Johnson, Bessie McClellan, Lucile Carpenter, and Mary Owen.

Journalistic training was afforded by the school annual, *The Beacon,* which first appeared in 1914 and was supplanted by *The Wildcat,* the present annual. The *Elgin Courier* allotted a page for editorial writing and school news from time to time, and *The Echo,* a system-wide mimeographed paper, enjoyed wide circulation, the elementary school students reporting as "the Little Rascals."

An athletic program was added to the system's academic courses in 1910, for physical training and participation in competitive sports by both boys and girls. Little enthusiasm was shown by the townspeople in those early matched games with other schools, but school spirit ran high when students watched "the dear old colors, brown and white, sailing around the diamond."

E. A. Jones was instrumental in organizing the school's first six man football team in 1913. The team, composed of Woody Davenport, Louie Pfeiffer, Travis Kimball, Jim Moore, Tom Taylor, Willie Head, Don Gillum, Clay Davis, Willie Griffin, and Marvin Standifer, was coached by J. C. Welsh. The same group appeared later in the season as a baseball team. The athletic department grew, and 1915-16 included a track team which was successful in Interscholastic League competition. The baseball team the same year triumphed over some arch rivals of today, winning over Bastrop and Smithville, but losing to Giddings. The team composed of Jim Moore, John McCall, Archie Owens, Erwin Lanfear, Gordon Harris, John Sellah, Tom Taylor, Woody Davenport, Willie Head, and Curtis Sowell, won five games and lost three.

In 1915 the first girls' basketball team was organized. The senior team wore huge bows in the hair, with white middy blouses and voluminous bloomers which anchored their black ribbed stockings. The junior girls, to distinguish their uniforms, substituted wide-billed caps for the hair bows. The members of the senior team were: Marjorie Meeks, Olive Jackson, Ruby McCall John Mary Roemer Georgia Kincaid, Lucile Carpenter, Winifred Buchanan, Lillie Beth Wilson, Martha Bassist, and Lucille Johnson; the junior team included Ruby Lanfear, Esther Parnell, Rachelle Torno, Lou Ella Stowers, Zelma Prewitt, Adelle Hughes, and Winnie Head. By 1917-18 the team chalked up a victory of 4-3 wins when coached by Miss Virginia Eleanor Rootes. The Letter *E* was awarded to Ruth Casey, Thelma Fitzpatrick, Tannie Taylor, Florence Mathis, Jewell Sturdivant, Marina Samuelson, and Annie Mae Gage in recognition of "their skill and faithfulness in practice."

Another first for the athletic department was marked in 1917, when "Coach Shalk", F. C. Shalkhauser, raised the school's first football eleven to compete in out-of-town-games. The team won one game but lost to rival Bastrop. "Shalk's" basketball boys had an outstanding year, however, winning all seven games they played. The baseball team, coached by Bill Brown with the assistance of S. M. Melton, won six of eight games that year.

Interest in football was slight in those early years as fans favored baseball, the "All American Game" of the time; but by 1937, interest in the game had grown to the extent that Elgin boasted a fenced and lighted playing field, paid for in part with money raised by interested citizens, with gate receipts buying equipment for the team. Coach J. C. Koen's Wildcats prepared for the season with a 10-day training camp at the brickyards that year, where football fundamentals were taught, fishing was enjoyed, and vast amounts of food consumed. In one outstanding game that season, the Elgin team was named winner in a tie game with Giddings, having gained more yardage and made more first downs.

Elgin football teams continued to distinguish themselves through the 1940's and 1950's under Coaches K. H. Thormahlen, Floyd Mechler, Burris Johnson and Melvin Crawford.

The Wildcats again tallied numerous wins under Coach Thormahlen, winning the district championship in 1953 and tying for it in 1957. In 1958, the team, coached by James Lyda, was Elgin's first to win bi-district championship, to go to region and win, to defeat the Mart Panthers in the quarter-final game at Temple, to defeat George West in semi-finals at New Braunfels, and finally to play for the state championship against White Deer at Sweetwater on December 20, 1958. Football spirit ran high and chartered busses filled with fans followed the team to the out-of-town games. A chartered plane, as well as busses, carried many to Sweetwater. A caravan of cars was led to the game from Elgin by Highway Patrolman Tommy Mosely. Though Elgin was defeated by White Deer for the championship, her pride in her team was not diminished. For "his feat of guiding an unsung Elgin High School squad to the Class A finals" Coach James Lyda was named Coach of the Year by the Texas Sports Writers Association.

In the 1930's Elgin High School Band began to march during the half-time period of football games. Besides furnishing entertainment at Elgin's athletic events, the band has given concerts throughout the years, marched in various local and out-of-town parades, and furnished entertainment for community affairs. One of its early members, Milton Dusek, in this year 1972 is completing his twenty-fourth year as director. The band now has a membership of seventy-two in High School, forty-nine in Junior High, and twenty-four in the elementary grades.

The pep squad has always stirred enthusiasm and support at athletic contests, and Elgin is especially proud of her "Purple Flames" drill team today. Other student organizations which have contributed to the development of students are the Future Homemakers of America, the Future Farmers of America, the Beta Club, the Science Club, and the Spanish Club.

The celebration of Elgin's one-hundredth anniversary, the ninety-eighth of the opening of the first school, and the seventy-fourth of the Elgin Independent School District, causes former students to pause in retrospect, tinged with nostalgia. For gone from opposite poles of the campuses are the two frame outhouses so surreptitiously overturned each Halloween night, only to be uprighted so publically under the stern supervision of the principal the morning after. Gone are the above ground cisterns and wells surrounded by boys and girls waiting their turn to drink from a freshly-filled bucket of water; gone are wood sheds and coal bins, the boys with arms or scuttles filled with fuel to warm the schoolhouse, and the girls with brooms to clean the class rooms; gone are the ponies tied to the hitching posts, waiting to hear the dismissal bells, and with them the horse barns, a favorite spot at noon to trade an apple for a fat garlic sausage.

Gone also are the exchange of chinaberries, rocks, and name calling between the boys at North School and the boys at Washington School, and the rivalry and keen distrust that existed between students at the North and South elementary schools. Gone are many students who trudged over rough walks to school, to stand in long lines awaiting orderly march to class; gone are the cloakrooms, and the water bucket and dipper placed so invitingly and conveniently at the back of the room, and the rows of triple, double, or single desks, screwed firmly to the floor.

The books, too, are gone: the *McGuffey Readers, Seaside* and *Wayside Readers, Pennybacker's History of Texas,* Sutton and Bruce and Sutton and Kimbrough arithmetics and Wentworth's algebra and geometry texts. And finally, gone is the musical sound of the clapper bell at four o'clock, dismissing school.

The town of Elgin will continue to look to its schools to prepare its young people to cope with and preserve the ever-changing environment. May the School Song's words linger long in memories as a challenge of loyalty to the past, and hope for the future:

"Oh, Elgin High forever
Firm together stand
Comrades true and faithful
Stand a league—we'll face the world so fearlessly
And true, the days that follow,
We'll pledge our loyalty
For Purple and White and all our might
We'll fight for victory"

Students in 1897 in the school in the old Masonic building, located opposite the Methodist parsonage.

1898 German class, taught by Professor Bolle in the old Masonic building. Front row: Othelia Benke, Freda Hecht, Olga Franke, Bertha Landman, Bertha Hecht, Anna Hecht, Lena Krueger, Ella Moehring, Minnie Neidig, Sophia Benke, Alma Moehring, Ella Landman. Standing between rows: Ollie Pfeiffer, Jessie Pfeiffer, C. F. Hanke, F. J. Hanke. Standing back row: Walter Voss, Alfred Benke, Joe Gunter, John Mogonye, Mike Mogonye, Albert Neidig, Otto Krueger, Herman Bahn, Will Moehring. Standing in back: Professor Bolle.

Students attending old red brick South School in 1921. School was built in 1897.

Mexican School in 1921, taught by Eduardo Lopez. Later another school was built on Williams Street.

Old Washington School, built in 1925.

Elgin High School, built in 1926.

Elgin football team that played in the state finals in 1958.

X CHURCHES

The centennial story of the religious life of Elgin had its foundation many years before 1872. As Austin's colonists came to Bastrop County, they brought along their religious faith, so greatly needed when leaving the safety of their homes back in the United States, to come and face the dangers of the frontier. The first services were rare events, but pioneer preachers, who came to the area, preached at log cabins where neighbors gathered to listen. Denominational lines were forgotten in the desire to hear the Word of God. Indian raids frequently broke up the services; so, wherever they went, many preachers carried guns as well as Bibles in their saddle bags.

The first church organized in all Bastrop County was the Methodist Church in Bastrop in 1833. One of its eleven charter members was Mrs. Mary Christian, later Burleson, who in 1840 was the first white person with a family to settle within the present bounds of Elgin.

As the county became more thickly settled, small churches were built in many rural areas. Some of these were Colorado Chapel, Osborn Chapel, the Perryville Baptist and Methodist Churches, and the Young's Prairie Christian Church. Pleasant Grove had Baptist, Methodist, Christian, and Presbyterian congregations. Numerous stories are told of the summer Camp Meetings held on Sandy Creek near Carr Springs, the place where Elgin's water wells are located. Often through the joint efforts of the various churches, revivals were held and many of the converts became leaders in their individual churches. The Methodist Abe Mulky revival in 1905 added 92 new members to the Methodist Church, 13 to the Baptist, 6 to the Presbyterian, and 5 to the Christian. The Presbyterian Lockett Adair revival in 1909 added 93 to the Methodist, 24 to the Christian, 17 to the Presbyterian, and 5 to the Baptist. In the Baptist Ham-Ramsey revival in 1913, 96 were added to the Baptist, and 75 to the Methodist. The Baptist Starnes revival in 1922 added 144 to the Baptist, 23 to the Methodist, 9 to the Christian, and 6 to the Presbyterian.

Ministers and laymen who participated in the Lockett Adair Revival in 1909. Top row: R. S. Deener, James Keeble, Carl Carlson, W. H. Kennedy, J. F. Meeks, W. E. McCullough, J. C. Miller. Bottom row: Rev. W. H. Turnage, Baptist pastor; Rev. Robert Paine, Methodist pastor: Rev. Lockett Adair, Evangelist; Rev. S. H. Comer, Presbyterian pastor; Rev. Nat B. Reed, Presiding Elder.

Ham-Ramsey Revival held in the old skating rink in 1913.

Early baptizing at Hanke Gin tank in 1912.

Winter scene, 1909, showing new Presbyterian Church building on right and Baptist Church building on left, built in 1884. Also shown are homes belonging to C. A. Martinson and Mrs. Lula Enders.

Mt. Moriah Missionary Baptist Church was organized at Pleasant Grove Community under two oak trees in 1879. This building was erected on the present church site in 1901. Rev. J. H. Winn was the pastor. The building burned in November 1938 and was rebuilt in 1939. Rev. H. D. Cummings was the pastor.

The Committee, with the assistance of local members, has compiled the following brief histories of the various churches in Elgin.

ELGIN UNITED METHODIST CHURCH

The Elgin Methodist Church, organized in 1874 in the newly built town subscription school located on the large lot opposite the present (1972) parsonage, was the first church established in the newly found town of Elgin. Meetings were held there until 1882, when a traditional one-room frame building with bell-tower and steeple was built on the site of the present sanctuary. In 1905 erection of the present cream brick building with its beautiful memorial art-glass windows was commenced at a cost of $10,000.00. Rev. L. C. Mathis was the then pastor; Building Trustees were John S. Smith, W. H. Rivers, H. B. Smith, A. H. Carter, and James Keeble. J. C. Miller was the Contractor.

Many early members came from nearby Perryville to the South and Pleasant Grove to the Northeast, including members and relatives of the Rev. Wm. I. Rivers (chaplain in the Confederate Army and early day Circuit Rider) and Mary Christian Burleson, who with her seven children moved to her Thomas Christian headright here in 1840. She died in 1870, but the influence of her life continues—one of her direct descendants, Mrs. Kittie Cain Henderson, is still a member here. Two of her great grandsons, Bishop A. Frank Smith and Bishop Angie W.

Smith, Elgin natives, for decades ably served all Methodism as spiritual leaders and administrators.

Trustees when the church property was bought in August 1882 were: John S. Smith, A. H. Carter, G. R. Davis, J. I. McGinnis, J. J. Sapp, J. M. Ransome, and J. Angerly. Early Ministers thru 1916 included such stalwarts as Revs. John M. Whipple, H. M. Haynie, S. H. Morgan, C. H. Brooks, E. G. Hocutt, L. C. Mathis, Robert Payne, J. C. Wilson, J. D. Scott, and J. E. Lovett.

Church improvements and additions have been made thru the years: 3-parsonages in 1883, 1909, 1950; a large 2-story brick Annex in 1923; Frame educational building 1949; brick Fellowship Hall 1958; central heating and air-conditioning came later.

Thru work among Latin-Americans begun in 1924 by Mrs. E. R. (Ned) Carter and Mrs. Lucy J. Rivers, progress was made, and in 1956 a new brick *Bethel Methodist Church* was dedicated. In 1962 its brick parsonage was built. Rev. Marta Rye is the current pastor; membership is 59.

As in all small churches, women of the congregation are a vital force in such. At Elgin they began with a Ladies Aid Society; in 1900 they added the Women's Foreign Missionary Society; later, the two groups combined. Membership now is 80 plus 17 shut-ins. Last year at their Annual Xmas Bazaar they netted $876.92, with such they contribute to mission work, church plant and parsonage niceties, etc. Mrs. Jack Webb is now president of the W.S.C.S. and Mrs. Ben Osborn, chairman of the morning circle. Sunday School, Methodist Men and Youth Fellowship currently are also functioning with Methodist groups.

Generous Memorial gifts have greatly enhanced the beauty and value of church facilities: $5500.00 W. H. Rivers electric pipe-organ (1925); Drs. King and Nofsinger oak communion table; $30,000.00 Lucy J. Rivers Endowment Fund (1930); Dale Willson motion picture projector equipment; Carl and Anna Martinson Annex improvements; Elmo and Ruth Condron Pastor's Study; C. W. Webb (1961) and Jerry Stach (1971) Sound system with 4 pews and other extensions; Mrs. L. R. Erhard-Ray Arbuckle outdoor masonry bulletin board and lighted redwood cross; K. F. Lane brass collection plates; W. H. Rivers, Jr., specially built four cathedral front doors and harmonizing companion electric lanterns; also cut-stone front steps with graceful ornamental handrails; Nell Owens Library and Memorial window; Lucy (Mrs. W. E.) Wood three panel art windows; Manda Methodist Bell monument; Eli Aronson Yamaha Baby-grand piano; A. J. Caldwell entrance registration desk; Sydney Laird-Henderson Brock sanctuary wall-to-wall and pulpit carpeting, with harmonizing green velvet pew cushions. In addition, there have been numerous other individual gifts including a Methodist Scholarship Fund of now $3,226.00 with its annual income going to an outstanding Elgin High graduate, who was active in church work in his/her last two years.

Several very Special occasions have been observed by the church during the 20th Century: in 1900, it advanced from Circuit to a full-time Station. In 1907 Bishop Seth Ward preached at the Dedication of the debt-free sanctuary; in 1939 they had Homecoming Day when original Church Bell was secured by Mayor R. L. (Bob) Carter and placed in the belfry of the brick church. In 1943 Methodist World War II Service Flag gave names of 27 of its youth including 2 young women; in 1945 they had Bishops Appreciation Day with unveiling of walnut wall plaque having gold letters honoring Elgin's two distinguished sons: Bishops A. Frank and Angie W. Smith, both of whom were guest speakers during the day. In 1955, the church observed its Golden Jubilee. In 1967 they had Manda Bell Memorial Day with Mrs. C. W. Webb as Chairman, dedicating the Bell used in early nearby rural Manda Methodist Church discontinued in 1962, and honored its pioneer leaders and members.

Present officers and Trustees are Philip Knowles, Chairman of the Board, Joe W. Meier, Ray Arbuckle Sr., George Johnson, Raymond Johnson, David Swenson, Wesley Niebuhr. Church Budget is $24,-239.00 with pastor's salary at $6,600.00 plus $300.00 for utilities and $1,200.00 travel allowance. Sunday School enrollment is 157 in 12 classes; Milton Saxon is its Superintendent. Methodist Youth Fellowship has an enrollment of 19; Messrs, and Mesds. Tom Lockridge and Kenneth Kisamore are the counselors. The church has a parttime secretary, three choir directors—adult, youth and joint community, two nursery attendants, an organist, pianist and assistant organist, one caretaker, and two editors of the church's occasional publication.

Rev. Bob L. Blackwell is the current pastor. Membership is 362.

MT. VERNON A.M.E. CHURCH

On August 28, 1898, a few families in Elgin gathered together at Jerusalem School and organized the Mt. Vernon A.M.E. Church. Rev. George Brown was the first minister. A brush arbor located six miles from town served the congregation until 1902. Then in 1904, under the guidance of Rev. Eugene Anderson, the first frame church was built. This church was rebuilt in 1911. Early officers were: Will Smith, Jim Brown, Willie Johnson, Henry McShan, I. Dunn and S. English.

In 1925 under the direction of Rev. Rufus Mozers, the church was moved to town and erected where it now stands at 215 Church Street. Under Mozers' leadership, the membership increased in number and in zeal.

By 1943, chiefly through the leadership of Rev. A. W. Harvey, the church debt was cleared and a parsonage was built.

The following years saw the installation of restrooms, a pulpit, and pews. The years 1969 and 1970 were times of particularly great material growth for Mt. Vernon A.M.E. Improvements included the installation of a new floor, erection of a new cafeteria, the remodeling of the parsonage and painting of the church. Rev. Julia Frances is the pastor since November 1969. Present membership is 47.

FIRST BAPTIST CHURCH

All records of the First Baptist Church prior to 1923 have been lost, so one must use every means possible to piece together its earliest history. Elgin's first station agent for the Houston and Texas Central Railroad was John Gordon. His son-in-law, E. D. Durfee, was also employed by the railroad. Both of these men have been credited with organizing a Baptist Sunday School in his home in 1873. Other charter members of this group were S. H. Bragg, W. M. Chiles, Mrs. James Fisher, Mrs. Frank Meeks, and A. F. Brown.

A supplement to the *Elgin Courier* on February 24, 1910, stated "From the best information obtainable, the organization of the Baptist Church occurred about the year 1875. The old Perryville Church dissolved about that time and most of the members came into the Elgin Church." This article lists the pastors from organization until 1910 and includes some outstanding Baptists of that time.

The first name on the list is N. T. Byars, who organized the church. He had come to Texas in 1835, opening a blacksmith shop at Washington-on-the-Brazos. It was in his building that the Constitutional Convention met and drew up the Declaration of Texas Independence, March 2, 1836. Byars was ordained as a Baptist minister in 1841, and most of his ministry was spent in organizing churches over Texas.

The first pastor of the church was Adoniram Judson Holt, who was also the last pastor of the Perryville church. He pastored the Webberville church at the same time as he pastored Elgin. In 1877, the Associational Minutes of the Austin Association listed Elgin's membership as 43. In 1881, there were 84 members, and they shared a pastor with McDade. Several union revivals through the years greatly enlarged the membership.

Until 1884, the Baptists worshipped in the town's schoolhouse. That year they erected a small frame building on the corner of West 3rd and North Avenue C. It was used for thirty-nine years, being moved to the side of the lot in 1909 so that a parsonage could be built next to it. The present church building was constructed in 1923 at the corner of West 2nd and North Avenue B, and the Masonic Lodge took part in the ceremony of the laying of its cornerstone. In 1956, a new brick parsonage was built on the site of the old one. Other improvements through the years have been a Sunday School annex, air conditioning, carpeting, and redecorating of the church interior. The church's library and business office are on the first floor of the two-story tile building connected to the church with covered concrete walks. The library with its 1784 books is considered an excellent one for a small church.

Memorial chimes were installed in 1963 in memory of the many devoted Christians who through the years had worshiped in the church. These are played each afternoon at 5 P.M. Among other memorial gifts are the organ and the pianos.

In 1949 the German Baptist Congregation came into the church, and these members have been faithful assets. A Mexican Mission was organized in 1951 by Rev. Kenneth Sellers, and a church building was erected on Williams Street. A parsonage was purchased for it in 1962.

Since its organization, the church has had thirty-eight pastors, Rev. W. Ray Head being the present pastor since 1965. The membership is 738.

GERMAN BAPTIST CHURCH

As early as 1910, German Baptists in and around Elgin met in various churches and conducted their services in German. At different times they met on Sunday afternoons in the Presbyterian and Baptist church buildings. For a period of time the little Holiness Mission Church was their home, and here they held classes so as to pass on their heritage of German language and culture.

But, on February 6, 1921, the congregation of 24 people, under the leadership of August Klaus and John Sippel formally organized a congregation, later building a white frame church on the corner of South Avenue F and East 6th Street. Among the charter members were the Klaus, Leseman, Heineman, Sipple, Kiphen, Berg, Ginsel, and Schiller families. Pastors included: August Becker, L. Vogt, A. P. Schulz, J. E. Ehrhorn, and J. J. Lippert.

Their preachers came from Waco, Greenvine, and elsewhere to minister to them. Keeping church connections, however, proved difficult; and in 1949, the congregation disbanded and united with the First Baptist Church.

MT. MORIAH MISSIONARY BAPTIST CHURCH

The years between the establishment of Mount Moriah Missionary Baptist Church in 1879 and the turn of the century represented a period of major development. Presley George of the Pleasant Grove community gave a group of ex-slaves permission to use a piece of his property under two large oak trees for their place of worship. There, they soon built a small church. Pioneer charter members were: Hampton Moore, Hampton Watson, John Harris, Pete Colvin, Wesley Jerry, Margaret White, Catherine Dunn and Francis McGinnis. Pioneer deacons were Aaron White, Arthur Westbrook, and Adam Stalworth.

Rev. William A. Pendergrass was the first pastor. Another church was built, and in 1889 it was moved to where the Westbrook Memorial Gardens Cemetery now is. In 1891, some of their members, called Little Flock, branched off and built a church in Southwest Elgin near now Highway 290. It functioned quite some years, but eventually the remaining members came in with Mount Moriah.

The far-sighted pastors of Mount Moriah between 1900-25 emphasized youth and their educational needs. Rev. James Kelley was instrumental in launching a drive to aid Guadalupe College in Seguin, which several Elgin students got to attend. During this time, under Rev. J. C. Lott, a parsonage was built, pews purchased, and worship services changed from once to twice a month.

Financial and spiritual progress was had the next 25 years. The church was moved from the Cemetery lot to its present location on Church Street. Services were held four Sundays a month, and a Junior Church was organized—advances brought about by Rev. I. N. White, who served from February 1927 until December 1935. After the annex burned in 1936 and the church in 1939, services were held in Pleasant Bethany Baptist for about a year until a new frame church was built. The membership increased. At a revival held by Rev. E. J. Johnson who came in 1949, fifty-one new members were added. Rev. A. T. Thomas became pastor in 1954 and plans were made to build a new edifice. When Rev. R. A. Westbrook came in 1959 they had $4,066.00 in the Fund and on April 4, 1960, there was much rejoicing when the attractive commodious, well-equipped brick church was dedicated. In May 1967 a new $7,000.00 parsonage was built. Additional parking land adjoining the church has been purchased since then.

Church auxiliaries consist of: Deacons with James Bryant as Chairman; Trustees with George Fowler, Chairman; Sunday School with David Scroggins, General Chairman; B.T.U. (Adult, Junior and Primary); Choirs (Seniors and Juniors) with Willie Jones, Beth L. Hall as sponsors; Mission #1 and #2 with Vivian S. Bryant and Addie Madison as Presidents; Deacons' Wives, headed by Jessie L. Fowler; and Usher Board headed by Otis Owen. Rev. R. A. Westbrook is the present pastor, and the membership is 150.

MT. PLEASANT MISSIONARY BAPTIST CHURCH

Mt. Pleasant Missionary Baptist Church was organized by Rev. Wormley in 1888 in a small frame building on Piney Creek. Green Henington donated the land site for the first church building. Later, Rev. J. W. Winn pastored in the same building.

The congregation thrived, and in 1900 a larger building was erected, in which Rev. A. B. Bevins was pastor for sixteen years, retiring when his health failed. When Camp Swift was constructed, the building and the grounds were sold to the Federal Government, and the congregation accepted the invitation of the Zion Chapel Baptist to worship in its church for the duration of World War II.

After the War, under the pastorate of Rev. G. W. Stewart, the present chapel was purchased from Camp Swift and moved to its present site on the Bastrop Highway one mile from Elgin. Under the leadership of the next pastor, Rev. H. J. Carrington, the debt on the building was paid in full.

Through the tireless efforts of Rev. P. Townsend, who came in July 1964, the church membership increased. A public address system was purchased; the Townsend's Fellowship Hall with public running water was added; and restrooms were installed.

The new pastor is Rev. Matthew Carter, and the membership is 75.

PLEASANT BETHANY BAPTIST CHURCH

The Pleasant Bethany Baptist Church was organized in July 1905 by Rev. John Winn. Services for the new church were held under a tree until a brush arbor with logs for seats could be built. Early members included Mockerson Johnson, Walter Jackson, Sammie Wheat, Elbert Garner, Lula Green and Ella Cheeks.

In 1906, after the brick sanctuary of Elgin First Methodist Church was completed, Pleasant Bethany purchased its white frame building and moved it to the east end of Church Street. Later, another building was added, all of which the congregation rebuilt and enlarged in 1947.

After Rev. J. E. James became pastor in July 1960, repairs were made and restrooms and a concrete walk were added. But on New Year's Eve of 1967, the building, including new pews, a piano, an electric organ, 20 Bibles and pulpit furniture, was destroyed by fire. Only the faith of the members remained! The Masonic Lodge Hall then became the church home for over two years, during which time 38 members were added. A new brick air-conditioned, fully equipped structure was completed and dedicated on July 5, 1970, since which time Rev. James has baptized 23 new members, some of whom came through a mission revival sponsored by Sisters H. T. Penson and Ophelia Brown.

Auxiliaries of the church are its Sunday School; Senior, Youth and Tot Choir; Male Chorus; Mission No. 1; a Junior Mission, organized in the 1940's; Deacons' Wives; Usher Board and B.T.U. Among current officers are: George Hatch, Early Brown, Louis Brown, Samuel Dove, Sherman McBride, Haywood McNeil, Willie Dove, James Denmon, Robert Simms, Isaiah Jones, Searcy Simmons, Ola Mae Bishop, Myrtle Dove, Georgia James and Ruby Jean Simms.

The present minister is Rev. J. E. James, and the membership is 209.

WINN'S MEMORIAL MISSIONARY BAPTIST CHURCH

Winn's Memorial Missionary Baptist Church was organized in 1933 by Rev. John Winn. Under his leadership, worship services were held in a tabernacle with a dirt floor until they built a small church, which was later replaced by the present much larger one, purchased from the Elgin Church of Christ under the pastorate of Rev. Clarence H. Means. The growth of the church was constant. In 1970, they listed five special accomplishments—purchasing robes for the choir, carpeting for the aisles and pulpit area, a water fountain, a piano, and a church bus.

The present minister is J. R. Williams; and the deacons are Perry Russell, James Martin, Lewis Nash, Owen M. Upshaw, J. D. Collins, Ernest Thompson and William Penson. Present membership is 104.

MT. CARMEL MISSIONARY BAPTIST CHURCH

Responding to requests by two blind parishioners, Dave Duvall and Grandview Parks, the Rev. A. H. Brown on January 13, 1952 with seven Charter members, organized the Mt. Carmel Missionary Baptist Church. Other charter members were: Dallas and Molly Duvall, James Canada, Andrew Owens and Ida Perkins. Brown was succeeded in 1957 by Rev. Q. S. Goins, present pastor.

Functioning auxiliaries of the church include a Sunday School, Senior Mission, Mission No. Two, Choir, Pastor's Aid, Brotherhood, Prayer Band, Baptist Training Union and Usher Board. The church is associated with St. John's Baptist Association at Austin and the Missionary Baptist General Convention. Present officers are: Ike Everett, Chris Floyd, Miner Thomas, Leroy Colvin, Morris McAthur, William McArthur, J. B. Brown, Jr., Mary Jane Richardson, Myrtle Duvall, Bernice Colvin, Myrtice Thomas, Mary Barker, Dorothy McArthur, Rosa B. Clarkson, and Molly Nell Goins. The Church has 90 members.

FIRST PRESBYTERIAN CHURCH

On April 10, 1881, Elgin's Cumberland Presbyterian Church was organized by Rev. A. J. Adkinson with charter members: P. E. George, L. J. George, Mary Biggs, G. J. Meek, W. F. Chiles, Josephine Chiles, E. J. Evans, J. F. Jackson, M. A. Speegle and James D. Newton. The church was admitted under the care of the Colorado Presbytery in October of that same year to be known as the Elgin Congregation of the Cumberland Presbyterian Church. Owning no church property at this time, the congregation gathered in various other churches and schools in the town, for services conducted by circuit-riders and part-time pastors.

Property was purchased on January 30, 1886, and a small white frame church and manse next door were erected. In 1888, Dr. A. D. McCullough, a minister of the Cumberland Presbyterian Church and also a dentist, moved to Elgin and was invited to supply the pulpit of the church part-time, which he did until 1897. The first Sabbath School was organized in 1890, with A. H. Decherd as superintendent and W. E. McCullough as assistant superintendent.

Rev. S. A. Comer accepted a call from the Elgin congregation on May 21, 1908, and with his family moved into the manse as the church's first full-time pastor. His officers were: W. E. McCullough, Dr. T. B. Taylor, J. S. Sharp, S. G. Linder, James Rucker, J. O. Perkins, W. M. Condron and Thomas Upchurch.

In 1909, the Elgin Cumberland Presbyterian Church became the First Presbyterian Church U.S.A. of Elgin. During that year, a new red brick veneer sanctuary was erected which is still in use today, with major restoration being made in 1971 on the outside and inside of the sanctuary.

From 1914 to 1933, the church did not have a full-time pastor, and the pulpit was filled by visiting moderators, pastors and laymen.

Mesdames Jesse C. Miller, Ed Fromme and Ott Arbuckle were the first officers of the Woman's Auxiliary, organized in January 1929. A series of student pastors from the near by Austin Presbyterian Theological Seminary served the congregation from 1933 to 1952.

In 1952 Jack Harrison was ordained in the church and became its first full-time pastor since 1914. He served until 1954, when students again filled the pulpit. The church observed its 75th Anniversary on April 8, 1956, with Dean James I. McCord of the Austin Seminary bringing the message.

A new educational building next to the church and a new brick manse on North Avenue C were dedicated on October 6, 1957. In 1960, the church became a part of the Rolling Hills Presbyterian Parish where two or more churches are served by one minister. Rev. Wilfred Galbraith, who resides in Elgin, now serves the Elgin and Giddings congregations, with Elgin having 67 members.

CENTRAL CHRISTIAN CHURCH

Many early settlers in this vicinity who were members of the Christian Church attended services at Young's Prairie, some 5 miles South of present Elgin. However, after the founding of Elgin, some of these members moved to town. In 1888, an evangelist, Rev. B. B. Sanders, conducted a revival in the Presbyterian Church and organized the Central Christian Church, which grew to 45 members, and met in the Presbyterian building until 1892 when its own church building was erected. Members named in the deed were: J. H. Litton, J. H. Wallace, A. H. Cole and W. Fite.

The Galveston storm of 1900 completely demolished the building and its records. A new building was built on the same site, but this was destroyed by another storm in September, 1915. The Presbyterians again shared their building with the congregation until a new white frame building was erected in 1916. During this period, Rev. C. B. Craig was pastor.

By July 1936, the congregation was composed of 68 members; Rev. Ralph Wolfe became pastor and during his pastorate, the memship doubled, making the erection of an Education Building necessary to provide rooms for the increased attendance in Bible School. The 2-story structure, built of tile, and dedicated November 20, 1938 joined the back of the sanctuary and was called "The Annex".

On May 15, 1941, the congregation purchased a nice frame house across the street from the church to be used as a parsonage. This was sold, when in 1956 a new brick parsonage was built on Lexington Road.

Under the leadership of Rev. William B. Reeves, a lovely well equipped, air-conditioned brown brick church with a beautiful ceiling-high stained art glass window was erected; and on September 12, 1965 the dedication service was held. The present pastor is Rev. Carroll Weedon. Membership is 85.

FIRST CHRISTIAN CHURCH

On July 4, 1970, a group of 55 Christians met in the Club Room of the Sunset Cafe for a luncheon and to discuss methods of organizing a new Christian Church in Elgin, led by Dennis Snowden, Chester Newman and Virgil Rabb.

One of the first problems was to secure a minister; two were present for this first meeting. Richard Robison, a student at Texas University and former missionary to Brazil, was selected to serve the congregation until May 1972, when he and his family will go to San Juan, Puerto Rico, where he will become Dean of International Christian University.

Formal organization of First Christian Church, with By-Laws and Incorporation Papers, was soon completed under the supervision of elders, deacons and officers chosen for this purpose, and through the courtesy of the Seventh-day Adventist Church, First Christian congregation has worshiped in the Adventist church building ever since. Plans are underway, however, to erect their own church building in the near future. The members pride themselves that 12% of the gross income of the church is given to four world-wide missionary projects. Its church membership is 53.

THE HOLINESS BAND

On November 1, 1900, a plot of ground was purchased by "members of the Holiness Band, residing in the town of Elgin, Texas and elsewhere . . .; said Holiness Band being an inter-denominational religious association composed of the members of various religious denominations and their sympathizers who endorse and practice the doctrines taught by the believers in Holiness." So reads the Deed to this land. The trustees named were J. D. South, and Mesdames Mary E. McDavid, Anna Speegle, S. E. Gober, and M. A. Clopton. The Little Mission Church, as it was called, was located on the triangle in the 400 block of McDade Road.

At times, other congregations, who had no house of worship, also conducted services there. Among such were the Universalists, the Lutherans and the German Baptists.

On June 11, 1911, the building and grounds were sold for $600.00 to the Church of Christ with Charles Gillespie, J. B. Martin and L. H. Scarborough as Trustees. By 1920, the building was no longer in use.

SACRED HEART CATHOLIC CHURCH

The Fathers of the Holy Cross were among the pioneer missionaries at Elgin. From 1908 to 1911, Father Mariano Majado and Father Jose

Sauz, C. M. F. served in this area. Pablo Rosas, as the lay leader, collected funds to buy a lot for the first church. Much of the labor to build the church was done by its members, with others in the community helping. The first church, located near the corner of North Avenue A and West 2nd Street, was dedicated to the Sacred Heart.

In the early part of 1912, the Oblate Fathers from Houston took charge and served from there. In 1924, Father DeAnta enlarged the building and built a sacristy. In 1925, Elgin became a part of the Guadalupe Parish in Austin, and in 1938 was transferred to Our Lady of Guadelupe in Taylor.

On June 6, 1945, Mr. and Mrs. Albert Mikulencak deeded some lots on West 11th and North Avenue B as a new location for the church. A chapel from Camp Swift was moved to this location and dedicated July 5, 1948.

In 1951, the Sacred Heart Church was promoted from the status of a mission to that of a parish. A new convent for the Catechist Sisters of St. John was built in 1955, and they resided here a number of years. In August of 1955, the church burned; but a large new brick building was erected at the same site, and dedicated in February, 1957. Recent improvements have been made, including the renovation of the large recreation hall.

Father Everett Trebtoske is the present priest. The church membership is 900, including baptized infants and children.

CHURCH OF CHRIST

No one is living today who was an active member in 1920, so little is known of the history of the Elgin church prior to then. However, there was a congregation of Disciples that met in Elgin prior to 1920, for on June 11, 1911, they bought the little Holiness Mission building located somewhere in the triangle in the 400 block of Old McDade Road. Trustees for the church listed on the deed were Charles Gillespie, J. B. Martin, and L. H. Scarborough. This building was gone by 1920.

By about 1921, Brother Luther Norman was preaching to a group who met in the Christian Church building on Sunday afternoons. Later, this group met over the old State Bank building, then in the Presbyterian Church, on Sunday afternoons. M. L. Singleton, J. D. Bailey, and Jim Taylor were among the men who were active in leadership during the 1920s and 1930s.

About 1929, the church purchased a lot on North Avenue C where the present building is located. A frame building was erected on this site and was dedicated on May 1, 1932. Dick Berry became the first located minister in 1950, but continued with his State employment job elsewhere.

In 1951 the church secured Ross Meredith as their first full-time located minister. He was followed in 1956 by Raymond DeSpain. A minister's home was purchased, and in 1958 the present modern brick air-conditioned church building was erected. A more adequate parsonage was secured in 1968. Gaston Welborn, who is attending the University of Texas Law School, is serving as the present minister. The church membership is 100.

ASSEMBLY OF GOD CHURCH

The Assembly of God Church was organized in 1917 by ministers Adkins and Southerland. Services were first conducted in the open air, but in the fall of that year a tabernacle was built with sides that could be raised or lowered. Mrs. Clara Jones was the first convert. Other early members were: Ida Smith, Leslie Hardwick, Mr. and Mrs. D. Taylor, Mr. and Mrs. Joe Shoemaker, Mr. and Mrs. Joe Shoemake, Jr., Mr. and Mrs. Walter McCaslin, Mr. and Mrs. George Pate, Mr. and Mrs. Allie Gardner, Mr. and Mrs. George Carnline, Mr. and Mrs. John Carnline.

In June 1919, a convention of the Assembly of God Churches was held at the Elgin church with about 200 ministers in attendance.

The present church building on South Central Avenue was constructed in 1949 with the ladies of the church assisting in financing the project by doing quilting for the public. On June 19, 1951, a dedication service was held, and the note on the building was burned. Rev. E. L. Carter is the present pastor. The membership is 25.

ST. PETER'S EVANGELICAL LUTHERAN CHURCH

During the latter half of the 19th and the early part of the 20th century many German people immigrated from the northern provinces of Germany and settled in the Elgin area. Attempts were made by Lutheran pastors as early as 1905 to organize the Lutherans among the people into a congregation. Probably the first service held in Elgin for them was conducted in the Union Railroad Station in 1905 by Dr. C. Weber. Other services were held infrequently until 1911. During that year Dr. Weber instructed and confirmed a small group in the old Central Christian Church.

On July 14, 1918, the St. Peter's Evangelical Lutheran Congregation was formally organized with the following present: Julius Werchan, Friedrich Klaus, Otto Klaus, Joachin Dablegott, J. Witte, Herman Fischer, J. Gest, Albert Neidig, a Mrs. Bahn, Hy. Bahn, M. S. Wenzel, Mrs. A. Nerkowski, Mrs. A. Schiller, Otto Werchen, A. W. Steger and W. F. Voelker. Rev. A. C. Koeppe was called as pastor.

In 1924, a building was purchased from the Rose Hill congregation, located northeast of Manor, and moved to the site of the present church on East 8th Street. Its formal dedication was held on September 7 of that year. A large segment of the Rose Hill members joined the Elgin congregation, thus greatly strengthening it. A new parsonage was dedicated on February 14, 1937. In 1944, a portion of the Siloah Lutheran congregation of McDade merged with the church. A Parish House became part of the church's facilities in 1949.

On March 1, 1953, the congregation voted to erect a new house of worship. A stately red brick sanctuary was completed and dedicated on November 22 of that year. In the summer of 1963 the church was air conditioned.

St. Peter's has had one son to enter tthe ministry, Rev. Willard Rother, who was ordained on July 16, 1961. The pastors from the time of organization are: Revds. A. C. Koeppe, F. Gerstmann, T. M. Haag, Herman Engeling, Jerry Thane, and the present pastor, Rev. James Witschorke. The current membership is 373.

GRACE LUTHERAN CHURCH

The origin of Grace Lutheran Congregation goes back to World War II when rationing made it more practical for one person to travel than a whole flock. The one person who traveled to serve that small flock of Lutherans in McDade, together with Lutheran soldiers stationed at Camp Swift, was the Rev. A. F. Michalk. He traveled from his charge in Fedor. When the war was over, services in McDade were discontinued, and the members attended services in Fedor and Manheim.

On January 28, 1951, services were resumed in McDade and conducted in the Siloah Lutheran Church of the American Lutheran Synod, which granted the Missouri Synod Lutherans free use of their facilities. The Post Oak Conference of the Texas District of the Lutheran Church, Missouri Synod, undertook this project as a missionary endeavor.

Under the leadership of Rev. G. Naumann of Manheim, on January 29, 1956, the members decided to move to Elgin and to call themselves the Grace Lutheran Church. They secured the facilities of the Seventh Day Adventist Church, which they used as their place of worship with Rev. Gustav Zoch of Taylor and Dr. M. Riemer of Concordia College in Austin, serving successively as pastors. Officers at that time were August Gruetzner, John Dube, Otto Gruetzner, Sr., Oscar Dube, and Robert Gruetzner. Leaders in their Women's Missionary League were Mesdames Otto Gruetzner, Sr., Oscar Dube, Harry Wuenche and Robert Gruetzner.

In November 1965, the congregation voted to have a church of their own and to erect a suitable commodious building on 11th Street at Highway 290. This was done and the dedication service was held on January 30, 1966. A neat brick parsonage was built on the same premises, and in February 1968 Pastor G. Heinemeier moved there and remained until his retirement in June 1970, shortly after the dedication of the Sunday School Annex. He was succeded by the present pastor, Rev. H. O. Hartfield. The church membership is 111. Current officers are Melvin Dube, John Dube, Damon Doss, Ervin Gustafson, Robert Gruetzner, Robert Carter, David Dube and John Anton Dube.

Leaders in the Women's League are Mesdames Ervin Becker, Victor Dube, Robert Gruetzner and Ervin Gustafson.

SEVENTH-DAY ADVENTIST CURCH

The Seventh-Day Adventist Church, was first started as a parochial school in the A. J. Jensen home in Elgin, with their three oldest children as the only students the first year. Mr. Jensen was an immigrant from Denmark, settling first in Chicago, then Kansas, where he married his wife, Miss Lou. By trade, he was a tailor; but after his conversion, he became a dedicated colporteur, going from place to place to sell Bibles and religious literature coming to Elgin in 1909. The first teacher of the school was an elderly man with a long beard. He lived in the Jensen home and they paid him $15.00 a month, plus room and board. By the fall of 1910, five other families moved here, and the school enrollment rose to eleven.

Their church Conference asked the Jensens to obtain land on which to build the school, so they purchased a farm some 6 miles East of Elgin, and on November 19, 1912 deeded some of the land to the Seventh-Day Adventist Church for a school and place of worship. They called the community "Pe Lee", the Hebrew word for "wonderful", which came to Mrs. Jensen in a dream.

The building erected there, served as the church and school until 1951, when the congregation on March 26th purchased a lot in Elgin on Lexington Road, and built thereon a nice brick edifice, their present church which they share with others when the need arises for a temporary place of worship.

For some years, the church had no pastor; so local elders, among whom were A. J. Jensen, R. B. Dunks, J. S. Thorp and J. H. Sylvester, served as leaders in their stead. One of the Jensen sons has said: "These men certainly knew and loved their Lord, and they loved to talk about Him loud and long. For us to sit in church for an-hour-and-a-half or two hours was nothing unusual! We enjoyed their enthusiasm, faith and down-to-earth counsel".

In the 1920's, the Conference began sending pastors for the Church. Their present minister is Jim Tucker, a layman doing graduate work at Texas University. The Church has 68 members.

EVANGELICAL FREE CHURCH

The Elgin Evangelical Free Church, 1205 North Avenue C, was organized when members and friends of the Kimbro and Type Churches, and representatives from the Texas District Society, met on July 9, 1954 at the Type Church to decide the future of both congregations. This meeting was necessitated by the fact that both churches had become too small in membership and attendance to carry on full-time work. A resolution was adopted to organize a new Evangelical Free Church in Elgin, and a committee was appointed to investigate the purchase of a lot and the expense of moving the building from Kimbro to this lot.

A second meeting was held at the Kimbro Church on July 23, 1954. Charter members were 32 persons from the Kimbro Church and 24 from the Type congregation. Officers elected were Carl Samuelson, Myron Swenson, Herbert Samuelson, Walter Gustafson, Eugene Lundgren, Ollie Gustafson, and Kermit Nygard.

On September 24, 1954, the Kimbro Church building was moved to their newly purchased two lots in Elgin, and the Dedication services were held May 1, 1955. A parsonage on North Avenue H was purchased in May 1-957, but was sold in 1964; and a new brick parsonage was erected by March 1965 on the lot adjoining the church property. In February 1971, a brick Fellowship Hall was completed. Rev. Paul Buckert is the interim pastor who succeeded Rev. Kenneth Bergstedt. Membership is 70.

This church record would not be complete without a brief history of the Kimbro and Type churches. Under the leadership of Gust Johnson and John Herner, ministers, a group met in the Smith School building on July 30, 1897, and organized the Kimbro Church with 37 charter members. Its church officers were William Smith, C. F. Berg, August Lind, and C. A. Sandahl. Nels Torn donated an acre of land on which the church was built. In 1944 this building was destroyed by a storm, but a new one was erected, and dedicated by Rev. Gust Johnson, who, 47 years before, had dedicated the first church.

On May 22, 1908, Rev. H. E. Sundberg, then pastor at Kimbro, organized the Swedish Evangelical Free Church of Type with 14 charter members. The first officers were Peder Nygard, Oscar Johnson, Victor Carlson, August Nyman, Alfred Jacobson, John Sunvison and Louis Nelson. A Danish member, Peder Nygard, donated the land for the church and a cemetery, and a building costing $700 was erected.

Elgin United Methodist Church.

Bethel Methodist Church.

Mt. Vernon A.M.E. Church.

First Baptist Church.

Mexican Baptist Mission.

Mt. Moriah Baptist Church.

Mt. Pleasant Baptist Church.

Pleasant Bethany Baptist Church.

Winn's Memorial Baptist Church.

Mt. Carmel Baptist Church.

First Presbyterian Church.

Central Christian Church.

Sacred Heart Catholic Church.

Church of Christ.

Assembly of God Church.

St. Peter's Evangelical Lutheran Church

Grace Lutheran Church.

Seventh Day Adventist Church.

Evangelical Free Church.

XI PROFESSIONS

PHYSICIANS

Elgin has never been a town for the nine-to-five doctor, for to practice medicine here one needed the stamina to see many patients, night or day, in town or miles out in the country. This town has been fortunate, for down through the years there have been those who have been faithful in the best Hippocratic tradition, ministering to the ill regardless of color, social status, or the patient's ability to pay.

One of Elgin's first physicians was Dr. Samuel Sheasby, a native of England who was born in 1834. After serving as a surgeon in the Confederate Army, he settled in Perryville in 1866, and in December, 1872, moved to Elgin, opening his office at the present location of Weed Instruments. He died in 1883.

Dr. George K. Young, a native of Virginia, also served in the Confederate Army, in Jackson's Brigade, and was in attendance after many of the major battles of the Civil War. After the War he set up his practice at Perryville, later moving to Elgin, where he died in 1882.

Another early physician who practiced first at Perryville and later at Elgin was Dr. O. G. McPherson, a native of Illinois. When Dr. McPherson lived in Elgin, his home stood on the present site of Meadows' Fashion Shop. One of his children, Mrs. Will Moehring, remembers much about Elgin's early history. Dr. McPherson died in 1884.

Dr. G. T. King, born in Tennessee in 1861, made his first professional call in Elgin on May 4, 1883. At that time he was practicing medicine in the Mount Pleasant community. Coming to Elgin on January 1, 1895, he bought the home and took over the practice of Dr. Samuel Cunningham. Dr. King died in 1944.

Dr. G. W. Cain, born in 1828 in Virginia, also served with the Confederate Medical Corps. It was 1885 when he began his practice in Elgin but lived only ten years after coming here.

There were numerous other physicians through the years. Some of whom were Doctors Spring, Martin, Harris, Bjorkman, Watson, Auler, Hudson, Mayo, Raybun and Atkinson.

Dr. T. B. Taylor, a native of Tennessee, practiced medicine in Elgin from 1902 to 1919. He later practiced in Bastrop and Jourdanton. When he died in 1950, his records showed that he had delivered 3738 babies during his medical career.

Dr. W. E. Wood, born near Elgin in 1879, began his practice in Paige, but came to Elgin in 1903 and practiced until 1955.

Dr. I. B. Nofsinger, born in Kentucky in 1864, came to Bastrop County in 1892 and practiced in McDade until coming to Elgin in 1906. His wife, the former Mary McWilliams, was a graduate pharmacist in their Old Reliable Drug Store, located where Meadows' Fashion Shop is presently located. Dr. Nofsinger died in 1938.

Dr. W. E. Campbell came to Elgin after World War I and practiced until 1956.

Dr. Julian Rivers, a native of Elgin, practiced in the 1930's but was killed in a car-train accident in 1934. Dr. Joe V. Fleming, a personal friend of Dr. Rivers, took over his practice.

Dr. Fleming, born in 1907, received his medical degree from John Sealy in Galveston in 1933 and was serving as house surgeon at Brackenridge Hospital, Austin, when he came to Elgin. He built Fleming Hospital and opened it for patients on April 7, 1938, fulfilling a lifetime dream. He constantly worked to improve his hospital, designing and helping to construct the air conditioning and heating system, an ice maker, and laundry. During World War II more patient rooms were added and an employee dining room built. In 1946 a second doctor's clinic was added. The waiting room had been enlarged and a pharmacy added when Dr. Fleming suddenly died on December 20, 1950, following an emergency operation in an Austin hospital for a duodinal bleeding ulcer.

Dr. Walter S. Moore had come to Elgin in 1946 and had set up practice in the second doctor's clinic, but in November, 1950, was called in the Navy. In January after Dr. Fleming's death, he was released because of the emergency situation existing and practiced here for two years before being recalled into the Navy. After serving his term in the Navy, he practiced medicine in Austin until his untimely death in the late 1960's due to a car wreck.

Mrs. Elsie Meier, who was in M. D. Anderson Cancer Hospital in Houston recovering from surgery at the time of Dr. Fleming's death, mentioned to Dr. Roy H. Morris, Jr., Senior Surgical Resident of that hospital, that she had lost her doctor in Elgin. On Christmas Eve morning, 1950, Dr. Morris drove to Elgin to see the hospital and to talk to Sam Culp, the business manager, Mrs. Fay Whitehead, office nurse, and Mrs. Joe V. Fleming. Being impressed with the facilities Dr. Morris decided he would like to do the general practice required here, so he agreed to take over Dr. Fleming's practice on January 1, 1951, and would practice in partnership with Dr. Moore. He saw his first Elgin patients on New Years Day as the town had been without a doctor for ten days.

Dr. Morris was born in Brownwood, Texas, in 1916. After finishing University of Texas Medical School in Galveston in 1944 and spending a year's internship and a year's residency in general surgery, he was on surgical service at Camp Hood, Texas. He then was a Hermann Hospital and later at M. D. Anderson Cancer Hospital, both in Houston, prior to coming to Elgin.

In June, 1964, Fleming Hospital was incorporated and called Fleming Memorial Hospital Foundation. The purpose of doing this was to make a non-profit foundation of the hospital. It now has twenty-three beds and many improvements have been made, including a sprinkler system and a new X-ray machine.

In 1964, Dr. Morris made plans for a new medical-dental clinic adjacent to the hospital. In September, 1965, the Medical-Dental Clinic of Elgin was completed and occupied. Its plan includes three doctors' offices, dentist office with complete equipment, laboratory, X-ray equipment and physiotherapy equipment.

Other doctors who have practiced briefly in Elgin in recent years are Dr. J. P. Chapel, Dr. Tom Lindstrum, Dr. Tom Reedy and Dr. Eugene Foster.

DENTISTS

Early in Elgin's history a dentist, Dr. Borden, came frmo Round Rock on regular visits. Dr. A. D. McCullough, also a Presbyterian minister, practiced dentistry from 1888 to 1897. Dr. W. M. Jones' office sign appears in an old photo of a downtown street scene. Dr. J. P. Tingle was here from 1897 to 1911 when he moved to Temple. Dr. W. E. Duff came later.

Dr. Leon Keeble began his practice in the summer of 1916. Born in Elgin in 1894, Dr. Keeble received his degree from Texas Dental College in Houston. His first office was located on Main Street in a suite of offices with Dr. Auler. In 1938, he built an office next to his home on North Avenue C. He died in 1959.

Dr. Charles Hughes practiced dentistry in Elgin for a brief period and left to continue his education. Dr. Charles Akin bought Dr. Hugh's equipment and practiced on Depot Street until 1965 when he opened his office in the Medical-Dental Clinic of Elgin.

CHIROPRACTORS

Dr. Mull was seemingly Elgin's first chiropractor. He was followed by Dr. Milton Sheppard, who was born in 1885 in Bastrop County, and graduated from Texas Chiropractic College in San Antonio. He was a practicing chiropractor in Elgin from 1926 until his death in

Fleming Hospital when first built in 1938.

Dr. Joe V. Fleming, builder of the hospital.

Dr. Roy H. Morris, Jr. and his staff in 1953. Front row: Mrs. Lena Weisner, Lolita Ochoa, Mrs. Xenia Bell, Mrs. Fay Carter, Mrs. Gladys Snowden, Mrs. Lula Mae Paris, Mrs. LaVerne Crawford, Mrs. Ida Mae Pate, Second row: Robin Kilgore, Mrs. Ruby Hickox, Mrs. Fay Whitehead, Mrs. Elsie Meier, Mrs. Lula Belle Reynolds, Mrs. Edith Peterson, Mrs. Wanda Retzlaff, Mrs. Ima Armstrong, Richard Swain, Mrs. Leatrice Jones. Third row: Arnold Retzlaff, Sam Culp, Mrs. Arbie (Branum) Fitzwater, Mrs. Annie Kreidel, Miss Bertie Truitt, Bill Rohlack.
Fourth row: Jack Kopecky, Dr. Ervin Berman. Fifth row: Dr. J. S Chapel and Dr. Roy H. Morris, Jr.

1949. His first office was in a downtown building but later he moved it to his home.

Dr. S. T. Warner, a graduate of Texas Chiropractic College, has practiced in Elgin since 1949.

VETERINARIANS

After graduating from Texas A&M College of Veterinary Medicine in June, 1951, Dr. Wallace H. Cardwell came to Elgin and opened his office downtown in the M. L. Rivers building. His practice grew rapidly, and he realized he needed space for pens for large animals and a larger facility for pet animals. Therefore, in 1953, the first Elgin Veterinary Hospital was built on South Main Street. Several local stockmen and interested individuals donated time and labor and helped arrange the loan to make the hospital possible. At this time, Dr. Cardwell was the only practicing veterinarian in Bastrop County.

In 1961, Dr. Charles W. Graham, also a graduate of Texas A&M College of Veterinary Medicine, became a partner in the Elgin Veterinary Hospital. It was soon evident that the two-man practice had outgrown available space. Again ground was broken for a new hospital, this time on a large plot on Highway 290. Open house for the new veterinary medical facility was held on Mothers' Day, 1962. In 1970, Dr. Ed Higgins came into the practice as an associate veterinarian.

The practice continued to grow and in 1971 was incorporated into three separate divisions. The first is Cardwell-Graham Veterinary Clinic, Inc. which handles the veterinary practice. The second is Southwest Stallion Station, and the third division is the Elgin Breeding Service.

LAWYERS

Elgin's first lawyer was Miles H. Hill, who according to the *Elgin Meteor* was there on May 1, 1880. He apparently came from Bastrop, where in 1879 he was listed as treasurer of a newly-formed "Bastrop Literary Club."

Judge J. E. B. Laird, a surveyor, lawyer, and former east Texas county judge, came to Elgin in the middle 80's. He and Hill practiced law in Elgin until their deaths, in 1911 and 1917, respectively. Ebb S. Hurt, son-in-law of former Texas Governor John Ireland, is listed as practicing in Elgin from 1890 to 1896.

C. W. Webb began practice in Elgin in early 1900, and was engaged in the law continuously until about a year before his death in January, 1961. He earned the title "Judge" early, having served for a few months as justice of the peace in 1901. In 1927, he was elected by the Bastrop County Bar to serve as district attorney during the illness of that officer, and he was later appointed special county judge during the regular judge's illness. He also served one term as a special district judge.

He served as Elgin's city attorney for 25 years, and was succeeded in that office by his son, Jackson S. Webb, who joined the family firm in 1947 after returning from World War II and receiving his law degree from the University of Texas.

Other attorneys practiced in Elgin, some of whom remained but a short while before moving on to bigger cities or wider practices. T. J. Lawhon came in 1901, S. J. Isaacks in 1903; J. H. (Jack) Hooker and P. C. (Powell) Maynard arrived in 1911; B. B. (Braxton) Wade and Amos Felts in 1913; Emma S. Webb, President of the Bastrop County Bar since 1969, came in 1923; Charlie Talbot in 1932; John L. Dannelley and his wife Ila N. Dannelley began practice in 1934.

Elgin's centennial year finds the community with three practicing attorneys: Jackson S. Webb, Emma S. Webb, and a 1960 arrival, Ross Meredith, who also serves as city attorney.

Judge C. W. Webb, 1877 - 1961 For over 60 years he was a leader in civic, educational, religious and legal activities of Elgin and vicinity.

XII ORGANIZATIONS

Social and fraternal organizations have been very much a part of the life of Elgin since its beginning. In 1874 an Odd Fellows Lodge was organized but discontinued later. In April, 1902, the Willard Richardson Lodge I.O.O.F. was organized with the following charter members: J. E. Rivers, William Owens, James Keeble, R. A. Carl, and J. G. Hanson. The year that it was discontinued is not known.

In the January 21, 1932, issue of the *Elgin Courier* is the account of Elgin's Rebekah Lodge No. 463 consolidating with Austin Rebekah Lodge No. 118 after a period of seventeen years of activity in Elgin. Members from Elgin attending the first meeting of the combined lodges were Mesdames Eva Dunbar, Clara Snow, Irene Horton, Olivee Wilson, Hallie Allen and Lena Finch.

DeMoley and Rainbow Girls were organizations for teenage boys and girls which were sponsored by the Masonic Lodge and Order of Eastern Star. The Woodmen of the World and Woodmen Circle had active lodges for many years.

Today the people of Elgin still enjoy the fellowship of fraternal and social organizations as the following accounts will show.

ELGIN LODGE NO. 328, A.F.&A.M.

Perryville Lodge was organized on April 10, 1869, at Perryville, Texas, in Bastrop County, about 2½ miles south of the present town of Elgin. It was chartered as Perryville Lodge No. 328, A.F.&A.M. on June 18, 1970. The Lodge building was used as a school house, church, and Masonic Hall.

When the Houston and Texas Central Railroad was completed from Brenham to Austin and the town of Elgin established, the members considered moving their lodge to Elgin and voted to do so in 1877. Upon moving, they met for a time in the upper story of a residence which was located about where 28 North Main is at the present time, then in 1880 they erected a building which was to be used jointly with the school. This was located across from the present Methodist parsonage.

In 1882 Perryville Lodge assisted in the laying of the cornerstone of the Bastrop County Courthouse. In 1897, the building on West 3rd being inadequate both for school and the lodge, it was decided to erect new buildings—the school building was the two-story brick structure on South Avenue C, and the lodge a two-story brick building on the lot now occupied by the drive-in section of the Elgin National Bank. The cornerstone of the lodge building was laid on November 30, 1897. Perryville Lodge No. 328, in order to associate itself with the town in which it was now located, voted on March 30, 1901, to change its name to Elgin Lodge No. 328. A third floor was added to the lodge building in 1911 which was used for the lodge meeting rooms, and the rest of the building was rented.

In 1920 Elgin Lodge celebrated its 50th anniversary with a meeting for Masons and their families on the lawn of the residence of J. C. Miller. In 1922 the building on the corner of North Main and 2nd Street was purchased, and the lodge moved to the upper story of this building in 1923. Permission was given from the Grand Lodge of Texas for Elgin Lodge No. 328 to lay the cornerstone of the Baptist Church on April 6, 1923. McDade Lodge No. 664 consolidated with Elgin Lodge on June 11, 1934.

The 75th anniversary of the lodge was held in 1945 on the athletic field of the High School. This was an open installation of officers of the Bastrop, Giddings, and Elgin Lodges, with the Grand Master of Texas installing the officers.

On September 14, 1964, the lodge voted to build a new Temple. The lots across the street from the post office on North Avenue C were bought, and the present building erected. The building was dedicated on October 25, 1965, in an open meeting by the Grand Lodge of Texas.

In 1970, Elgin Lodge celebrated its 100th anniversary. A barbecue was held at the V.F.W. Hall for Masons and families of Masons. The Ben Hur Shrine Band of Austin provided music for the occasion, and the Grand Master of Texas delivered the address.

EASTERN STAR

Elgin's first Eastern Star chapter was Elgin Chapter No. 45, which on September 11, 1886 was authorized by the Masonic Lodge here to hold its meetings in the Lodge Hall. Sometime later, this Chapter demised, and Dorcas Chapter No. 241, Order of the Eastern Star, was organized on June 8, 1904. It was constituted on October 12 of that year with the following charter members: J. C. Miller, Mrs. J. C. Miller, Maggie Roemer, Lula Tingle, Beulah Straus, Pearl Keeble, F. Keeble, Hattie Smith, Nannie Cain, C. A. Smith, Mattie Decherd, L. C. Davis, Dorcia Taylor, Minnie Jackson, Pauline Taylor, Sadie

McCullough, Bettie C. Wade, Hilda Nordlander, R. Roemer and J. S. Smith. Mrs. Hattie Smith was the first Worthy Matron, and Mr. J. C. Miller was the first Worthy Patron.

On March 1, 1927, the name Dorcas Chapter was changed to Elgin Chapter No. 241. All meetings, since organization, have been held in the Elgin Masonic Lodge Hall, and Chapter meetings are regularly held each second Thursday of the month. At present, the Chapter has 132 members, and is the largest Chapter in District 4, Section 8. Mesdames Ila Dannelley, Emma S. Webb, Irene Brown, Lena King, Lena Pfeiffer, Otillie Sowell and Ila Lane have been members over fifty years.

NEGRO FRATERNAL ORDERS

Ever since the turn of the century, the negroes of Elgin, in addition to their church activities, have endeavored through their various fraternal organizations to establish high ideals and charity and relief among their people. The "Free and Accepted Masons" have three such organizations in their circle.

Texas Advance Lodge No. 207 of Elgin, with its Most Grand High Court in Fort Worth, was chartered July 21, 1905 with J. H. Witledge, Worshipful Master; J. W. Patton, Senior Warden and Wm. Arthur (Bill) Westbrook, Junior Warden. Later Masters were: Greely Westbrook, Rev. I. W. Robinson, N. W. McDonald and Otis A. Owens, Sr., the present such officer.

Their first Sister organization, Heroines of Jericho, Ida M. Winn Court No. 92, was established on July 17, 1906 with Mrs. M. A. Witledge as Most Ancient Matron, Mrs. L. C. Henderson as Senior Matron, Littie Riller as Junior Matron and J. T. Riller as Joshua. Later Matrons were: Mary Wheat, Littie Riller, Vioila Wilson, Cora Fowler, Willie Chandler, Lula Patton and Jessie Lee Fowler, the present such officer. Later Joshuas were: J. T. Rillar, Marshall Wilson, Chauncey Martin and James Bryant, the present such officer. Some of their other early-day members included Caroline Westbrook, Lottie Hicks, Helen Baker, Mattie Clay and Etta Penson.

An Affiliate of the Heroines is Tiny Crest Palace No. 334, a juvenile group organized in July 1955 with Vivian S. Bryant as first Queen Mary; James Bryant Jr. as Ancient Prince; Harry Swain Bryant as Ancient Senior Prince; Ernestine Madison as Ancient Junior Princess and Shifton McShan as Father Joshua.

Their second Sister organization, Green's Delight Chapter No. 363, Order of the Eastern Star, organized by Mrs. Alma Green, received its Charter on June 25, 1948 with Blanche A. Robinson, Worthy Matron and Edward D. Johnson, Worthy Patron. Their Affiliate is a Youth Fraternity with Adella Bonner as present Youth Sponsor, Angella Bradley as Princess Matron and Arthur Blocker as Prince Patron.

In the early '60's, the above Free and Accepted Mason Family purchased the old Washington School property on South Side; and plans are now underfoot to erect thereon "an ultra modern, unique structure for the Masonic Family". Thru the years, their organizations have been participating in a Youth Scholarship program for 12 colleges and universities, which awards during 1971-72 gave $400.00 to each recipient. The Elgin members are proud that some of their local youths received signal honors through such Scholarship Awards. In 1966, James Bryant, Jr., won 1st Place in an Essay Contest and received a $750.00 Scholarship at the Masonic Grand High Court meeting held in Ft. Worth. In 1967, Harry Swain Bryant, a brother of James, won 2nd Place in a Contest sponsored by the Heroines and 3rd place in the Contest sponsored by the Masons—both Scholarships totaling $750.00. Then, in 1970, Hazel Clark won 1st Place in the Essay Contest. Her award was a $500.00 Scholarship.

Elgin's negro community has another Masonic group, with Headquarters in Austin, which they term "4-Letter Masons" (Ancient Free and Accepted Masons). This group has Robinson Lodge No. 16 with Samuel T. Dove as the present Worshipful Master and Rev. Q. S. Goins as Secretary.

Their Sister organization, Morning Star Chapter No. 14, Order of the Eastern Star, was organized October 15, 1906 with Mary Jefferson as Worthy Matron, Eliza Tisdale (now Harrison) as Secretary and John Ward as Worthy Patron. Ranking officers in 1972 are: Myrtle Duval, Worthy Matron; Etta Mae Brown, Associate Matron; Eliza Harrison, Secretary; Olivia L. Loving, Treasurer and Rev. J. D. Harrison, Worthy Patron. During its 66-years of operation, Morning Star has lost but 7 of its members by death: Mary Jefferson, Stella Williams, Gussie Houston, Annie Martin, Harriet Beck, Iva Mitchell and John Ward.

NEW CENTURY CLUB

Reading from the minutes of the first meeting of the New Century Club, we learn the following:

"On February 26th, 1897, a corps of ladies met at Mrs. M. T. Smith's for the purpose of organizing a Ladies Literary Union.

Miss Nara Brooks was chosen to take the chair and after some persuasion consented to keep it as our first President. Mrs. Hill was elected Vice-President and Mrs. Herschberger, Secretary. By decision of society we are to meet every alternate week at the homes of members taken in alphabetical order. Mrs. Smith, Mrs. Bennett, and Mrs. McMullen were appointed a committee to form the constitution and by-laws.

Mrs. Herschberger was ordered to send for pamphlets which she did but the order was not filled.

After completing the program for next meeting we adjourned to meet two weeks hence at Mrs. Mable Roberts'.

Lillie Herschberger, Sec."

Though charter members were not listed, the following were early members: Mesdames Bennett, O'Conner, Jeff Meeks, McMullen, J. W. Hill, G. T. King, M. T. Smith; Leon Keeble, Eugene Brooks, Jim Walling, Davis, R. P. Jones, Buck, Thomas, H. B. Smith, George Hill, R. B. Walling, Thompson, W. H. Carter, Emma House, W. H. Rivers, G. H. Jones, Torno, Mable Roberts, and Lillie Herschberger. Also Misses Moore, Florence Sheasby, Edna Sullivan, Maude Campbell, Jennie Campbell, Maude Watson, Lee Litton, Marie Stewart, Jennie Clopton, Jennie Jackson, and Nara Brooks.

The purpose of the culb was, and still is, the intellectual advancement of its members. At first the ladies met in the homes of the members, then in a downtown rented room. Afterward a home in the business section was bought and made into a club house. In 1949 a barracks from Camp Swift was moved in on a large lot on Lexington Road and remodeled into an attractive club house and is the present home of the club.

In 1921 the club became affiliated with the General Federation of Women's Clubs.

One of the earliest projects of the club was a library which was open to the public for many years. In 1953 it received a citation from the Library of Congress acknowledging the gift of newspapers: The Philadelphia Sun, dated April 17, 18, 19, 1845, and The Philadelphia

Early New Century Club members. Those pictured are: Mrs. Thomas O'Conner, Miss Tempie Newland, Mrs. Bob Jones, Mrs. W. H. Carter, Mrs. M. B. Keeble, Mrs. James Smith (Visitor), Mrs. Morgan T. Smith, Miss Jennie Clopton, Miss Jennie Jackson, Miss Maude Campbell, Mrs. G. T. King, Miss Lula McGinnis (Mrs. Leon Keeble), Miss Lee Litton (Mrs. S. J. Smith), Mrs. J. J. Bennett, Miss Jewel McCullough (Mrs. C. D. Speed), Mrs. R. L. Wilson, Mrs. Mabel Roberts, Miss Mary Stewart (Mrs. W. J. Buck), Mrs. J. W. Hill, and Roy D. Rivers, Leon Keeble, Ernest Carter, Children.

Press dated March 31, 1862. These were taken from its collection of old books.

Various honors and awards have been won by the club through the years. Some of these were the USO Award in recognition of Distinguished War Service, and the 1956-58 Community Achievement Contest sponsored by the General Federation of Women's Clubs and Sears Foundation.

The club has been entertained by many outstanding speakers through the years. It has always entered into all civic projects, working toward the betterment of the community. At this time, it has three honorary members, nine associate members, eight life members, and thirty-five active members.

ELGIN FIRE DEPARTMENT

As early as 1898 there was a group of volunteer firemen whose equipment was a cart with reel and hose, hook and ladder. A list of their officers included O. Rehfeld, Max Hirsch, W. I. Freeman, John Parnell, Tom Pfeiffer, C. Franke and R. A. Carl.

Through the years fires destroyed many homes and businesses. On October 2, 1898, the two-story City Hotel burned down. In 1909, several small businesses, located in the area of the present post office, burned to the ground.

Elgin Volunteer Fire Department in 1914. Front row: Herman Fischer, Emil Burke, Charlie Berg, Pat Burns, Otto Salcher. Middle row: S. Truitt, J. E. Buchannan, Fred Bones, Dutch Frazier, Arthur Morell, Robert Lehman, Joe Sandgarten. Back row: Max Kurth, Louie Deisch, George (Bud) Frazier, John Christensen, Axell Smith, Fritz Hanke, Coates Keeble.

First fire truck purchased in 1916.

Fire Station, owned by the Volunteer Fire Department, was built in 1925.

After Elgin acquired its water system in 1909, fire hydrants were available to help in the fire fighting, so on January 16, 1910, the Elgin Fire Department was organized with C. F. Berg as fire chief. Mr. Berg was so loyal to the department that when he died some years later, his casket was carried to the cemetery on the fire truck.

In 1911, after the department had been organized, four homes in the 100 block of West 7th Street were destroyed by fire. These were the homes of W. C. Brown, George Garrett, Will Moore, and John Jenkins. Rufe Taylor was baby-sitting in the Brown home and noticed a fire in a neighbor's house at about 9:30 o'clock. He gave the usual alarm of the day by shooting his gun several times in the air. Many of the young couples were attending an entertainment at the skating rink on the southside. On hearing the shots, all present rushed out to help. Most of these had to reach the site by walking or running. The city's two-wheel cart did not have enough hose to reach the nearest fire hydrant. The city water pressure was low, so a bucket brigade was set up at the well on the corner of North Avenue C and West 8th Street, presently the home of Mrs. E. O. Lundgren, Sr.

During the year that Emil Burke was fire chief, his wife organized a ladies auxiliary to help in any way that women could. She was a great influence in getting a new fire station built in 1925. This two-story brick building, opened formally on September 8 of that year, provides upstairs living quarters for its dispatcher, while the lower floor houses the engines and equipment.

The first fire engine, bought in 1916, is kept in good condition and is a regular entry in all Elgin parades. It is a chemical truck, with solid tires, chain drive, and runs on a magneto. The department has three fire engines in which local and rural calls are answered. A resusitator is part of the equipment. Louis Hashem is the present firechief, Alvin Langhamer, assistant chief, and Rudolph Hoden, the dispatcher of the thirty-three member department.

ELGIN CEMETERY ASSOCIATION

On June 1, 1883, Mrs. Lee Gordon bought a plot of land from the trustees of the Houston and Texas Railroad. Her husband, John Gordon, the first station agent in Elgin for the railroad, had died on Christmas Day, 1882, and was buried in this plot. There were other graves already there, but there was some talk of the railroad moving these. Apparently it was decided not to move them as Mrs. Gordon bought the property for the cemetery for a sum of $200. Just a few weeks later, on July 25, 1883, she sold this acreage for the price she had paid to five trustees selected by the citizens of Elgin so that it might be used as a public cemetery. These trustees were W. P. Miles, J. I. McGinnis, F. R. Jones, F. R. Martin, and Miles H. Hill. A burial lot 45 feet long and 20 feet wide was reserved for the Gordon and Durfee families.

In order to enlarge the cemetery, some adjoining land was bought from Mr. and Mrs. J. Z. Hattox on November 1, 1952.

The exact year of the organization of the Cemetery Association is not known, but it is said that Mrs. William Owens was the first president and Mrs. J. W. Walling the first treasurer. Early caretakers were S. W. Wenzel, P. M. Rabb, and Alfred Brown. Mrs. W. P. Culp, Sr. sold the first cemetery lots. Various projects through the years have made the cemetery neat and beautiful. These projects have been the drives, the crepe myrtles that were palnted on either side of these drives, the cyclone fence, the guard light, and the new entrance gates.

THE UNITED DAUGHTERS OF THE CONFEDERACY

The William Owens Chapter of the United Daughters of the Confederacy was organized in Elgin on September 12, 1912 by Miss Katie Daffan during the Reunion of Terry Texas Rangers held here. Its Charter was received the following December 12th. Charter members were Mesdames William Owens, R. L. Carter, W. H. Rivers, Katie Scott, E. B. Wade, F. S. Wade, W. E. Wood, Henry Enders, Misses Nell Owens and Otnie Robinson. Mrs. William Owens, wife of the Confederate for whom the Chapter was named, was its first President.

The presidents through the years have been Mesdames William Owens, F. S. Wade, W. H. Rivers, Katie Scott, E. B. Wade, W. E. Wood, W. E. Duff, W. H. Carter, Ed Fromme, M. P. Dalton, M. L. Rivers, Harry Davis, Paul Farris, W. C. Brown, Bruno Ernst, A. A.

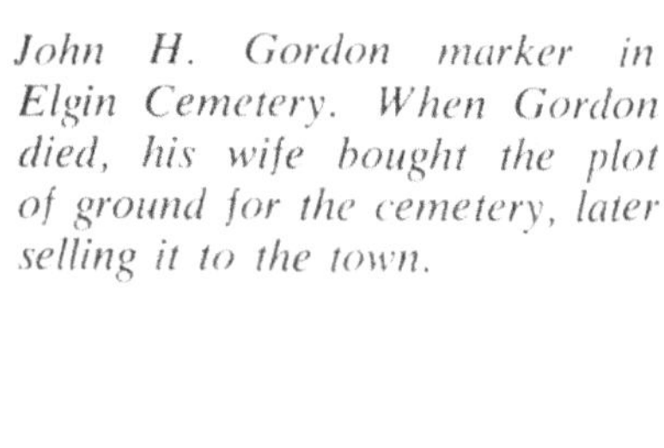

John H. Gordon marker in Elgin Cemetery. When Gordon died, his wife bought the plot of ground for the cemetery, later selling it to the town.

George, John Barton and R. G. Tullis, the present such officer.

In 1953, the Bastrop Chapter transferred into the Elgin Chapter. In 1938, Mrs. W. E. Wood organized the Anne Lee Chapter of the Children of the Confederacy. Many projects have been carried out through the years to honor those who fought in the Confederate Army and to perpetuate their memory.

THE AMERICAN LEGION

In March, 1921, Dr. W. E. Campbell, Edwin Lundgren and L. H. Barnes called a meeting of World War I Veterans. Twenty-five service men met March 26th and with the assistance of Col. John W. Young of Austin, District Chairman of the Legion, organized post 295, naming it Henry A. Lundgren Post for the first of our local heroes to fall in action in the great war.

Charter members were W. E. Campbell, A. J. Rankin, Roy D. Rivers, Louis Bahn, Henry Speer, Ollie Pfeiffer, W. C. Rivers, F. J. Hanke, John M. Casey, Adolph Sowell, L. H. Barnes, Martin Walberg, Sid McCall, E. N. Sowell, J. K. Boone, W. T. Dungan, H. G. Davis, A. H. Dungan, C. A. Swenson, C. E. Davis, B .A. Friedman, and Jennings Torno. The first meeting place was the Bassist Building on south side. There were 242 Elgin boys who served with the colors: 194 white boys and 48 colored.

One of the first local events in a civic way staged by the Post was July 4, 1921 when a big barbecue was held at Carter park for the purposes of bringing the Legion to the notice of the public—to acquaint the citizens with its aims and purposes, and to boost membership. All stood at attention from 11:58 till 12 noon in silence, facing west in reverence to the dead of World War I.

Through the years the Legion Post in Elgin has been engaged in aiding the widow and the veteran's families. Ever since Boys State was organized, Elgin has had one or two representatives each year. Patriotism and loyalty to country has been the positive program of the American Legion and always under excellent leadership, it has marched forward to an active, continuing strong arm of civic and American ideals.

Officers for 1971-1972 are Commander Erwin Roemer, Adjutant Jack Webb.

AMERICAN LEGION AUXILIARY, HENRY A. LUNDGREN UNIT NO. 295

The American Legion Auxiliary, Henry A. Lundgren Unit No. 295, Elgin, Texas, was organized in 1922 with seventeen charter members, Mrs. W. E. Campbell serving as President of the newly organized unit. Two of the charter members, Mesdames Edwin O. Lundgren and A. J. Rankin, have been continuous members until the current year of 1972, and they have been honored by the unit with fifty-year membership pens. The American Legion Auxiliary is one of the largest and most influential women's organizations in the United States. Currently, the Elgin unit has a membership of fifty, and Mrs. Erwin Roemer is serving as President. Through the years the Elgin unit has carried on all phases of the American Legion Auxiliary program, selling poppies to raise money for the rehabilitation of veterans and their families. Gifts have been sent to Veterans' Hospitals, and a program of Child Welfare has been carried on. One or two girls have been sent from this unit to Bluebonnet Girls' State each year.

Past Presidents of the American Legion Auxiliary, Henry A. Lundgren Unit No. 295, Elgin, Texas, include the following:

Mesdames W. E. Campbell, W. D. Nichols, Chas. Berg, A. J. Rankin, F. J. Hanke, E. N. Sowell, E. W. Felter, Kenneth Culbertson, Otto Larson, J. Ray Ivey, Pearl Keeble, E. O. Lundgren, John L. Dannelley, Wm. Conway, Dale Willson, Robert Johnson, J. C. Miller, Jr., Otis Schanhals, Jackson S. Webb, Pauline Swenson, C. W. Webb, Edwin O. Lundgren, Jr., Cecil Fisher, W. D. House, Chas. Joseph Poth, Lawson Rivers, Nell Owens, Ralph Lundgren, W. B. Foehner, Harvey Fisher, A. A. George, Roy Rivers, Jr. and Bernice Swenson.

ELGIN V.F.W. POST 6115

A charter was granted for the Elgin V.F.W. Post 6115, November 14, 1963, by the National Headquarters, Veterans of Foreign Wars, Kansas City, Missouri. Post meetings were held, prior to the building of a Post Home, at the Elgin Chamber of Commerce Building and at 106 North Avenue F the first Monday of each month.

Approximately 6.7 acres of land were purchased from Howard Rivers, III, on May 18, 1964, just off Highway 95, on Little Sandy Road, one mile south of Elgin. In September, 1964, on this property was built a 50' x 80' brick building, with kitchen facilities, a barbecue pit, etc. with a seating capacity of about 250. A formal dedication of the building was held March 28, 1965. An additional 10 acres were purchased from the same tract of land in June, 1965. In June, 1969, the building was enlarged to a seating capacity of about 400, with additional rest rooms, a larger kitchen and storage room.

The Post Home has been used for civic and social functions, and is available for such functions in the community.

Post Commanders

1963-1966	Cecil W. Fisher
1966-1967	Dale Cannon
1967-1968	Dimmitt White
1968-1969	Elmer Eklund
1969-1970	Dale Carter
1970-1971	Esten Williamson
1971-1972	Robert Owen

The Elgin V.F.W. Post 6115 Auxiliary was granted a charter on April 12, 1965. Auxiliary meetings are held the second Monday of each month.

Auxiliary Presidents

1965-1966	Lillian Fisher
1966-1968	Emma Jean Kisemore
1968-1969	Iris Cannon
1969-1970	Betty Lynn Meyer
1970-1971	Anna Belle Williamson
1971-1972	Lillian Fisher

BOY SCOUTS

Elgin's first Boy Scout Troop was organized about 1913 by Lyman J. Bailey of the Travis County Scout Council, with Judge C. W. Webb as scoutmaster, the first 20 members being boys from the Hikers' Club which Webb had organized in 1911. John E. Nichols recalls the splendid hikes and activities that they had. During World War I the troop disbanded; but on April 28, 1928, a new Boy Scout Troop was chartered with Richard Green as scoutmaster and Eli Aronson and Philip Walberg as assistant scoutmasters. The first Cub Pack was started in 1946 by Mrs. Elise Rivers and Guy Carter.

In 1947, under Scoutmaster Norman Dixon, Albert Payne Williams became the first native Bastrop County Scout to receive the Eagle Scout Award. In 1951, also under Scoutmaster Dixon, William F. Condron, Jr., James L. Condron, and Jimmy Lundgren received this master Martin McDonald, being the first Negro in the 15 county Capitol Area Council to receive it.
award. James Bryant, Jr. received this award in 1966 under Scout-

Scoutmaster Melvin L. Murphy had the pleasure to work with seven boys from Cub Scout age through the rank of Eagle. They were Carl Nall, Billy Voelker, and W. C. Murphy who received their awards in 1966; Mike Frase, David House, Paul Morris, and Byrd Murphy who received theirs in 1967.

Marvin Farrell received his Eagle Award under Scoutmaster W. M. Farrell in 1971. Mr. Farrell is the first Bastrop County Adult Scouter to earn the Wood Badge, the highest award given for training.

At the present time Troop 181 has 25 Scouts under Scoutmaster Oscar Ramirez; Troop 182 has 18 Scouts under Scoutmaster Farrell; and Cub Master Hardy England serves 35 boys in Cub Pack 182.

One of the most faithful Adult Scouters was Paul G. Lundrgen who served for 35 years in all capacities, both local and council wide. He was presented many honors, including the Silver Beaver Award in 1964. Adult Scouters to hold the Silver Beaver Award are Dr. Roy H. Morris, Guy Carter, and Martin McDonald. Dr. Morris is now serving as vice-president of the Capitol Area Council Executive Board and Mr. Carter serves as a member of the Board.

THE TEXAS LOST PINES RIDING CLUB, INC.

The Texas Lost Pines Riding Club, Inc. was formed on September 5, 1967, by the merging of the Texans Riding Club and the Lost Pines Riding Club, both clubs being located in Bastrop County. At the time of the merger there were 36 member families in the two clubs who were incorporated into the new club. The officers elected were:

President—Nig Hoskins
Vice-President—Carl Chambers
Secretary—Mrs. Mary Allison
Treasurer—Ervin S. Stuard
Drill Captain—Julius Marek
Co-Captain—Otto Wiley
Sweetheart—Nancy Parker
Refreshment Committee—Mrs. Evelyn Parker and Mrs. Otto Wiley
Reporter—Charles (Chuck) Stuard

The club met in the Elgin Police station for a year but now meets in the T.P.L. conference room on the first Tuesday of each month. A six acre tract of land was purchased just south of Elgin on Highway 95 on which to build an arena. The final stages of its construction will be completed by the time the town's centennial is observed so that its first rodeo may be held at that time.

In September, 1969, the club applied for and was granted a charter of incorporation from the State of Texas. Since that time each member has spoken with pride when mentioning the Texas Lost Pines Riding Club, Inc.

Trail rides and play days were the club's chief interest until the spring of 1969 when the club became co-sponsor with the Elgin Chamber of Commerce of what is now known as Elgin Western Day. Due to the success of the first Western Day, it has become an annual event.

Perhaps the best way to summarize the goals of the club is to quote from its By-Laws:

"The function of the club will be to . . . foster and promote the use of better horses and to keep alive the spirit of the old west. Also to promote a clean healthful environment for family fun and pleasure through the use of horses and other livestock, and to interest young people in our activities."

CHAMBER OF COMMERCE

The Chamber of Commerce received its charter on June 5, 1934. On May 24 of that year a group of thirty-two citizens of Elgin met and associated themselves together in an organization whose purpose it was to serve the interests of the community and to promote its commercial and agricultural activities. The first secretary was D. G. Flenniken who served in that capacity until his death in 1938. A list of the presidents and the years that they served are:

J. O. Smith—1934-35
Martin Walberg—1936-37
E. N. Sowell—1938
Virgil Rabb—1939-40
W. E. Gattis—1941
J. A. Freeman—1942
J. F. Metcalf—1943
A. H. Lovvorn—1944
V. E. Reimenschneider—1945-46
J. Z. Hattox—1947
Cecil Miller—1948
E. A. Woods—1949
M. L. Simon—1950
C. P. Morrison—1951
Chas. H. Fromme—1952
Dr. Wallace H. Cardwell—1953-54
W. E. Arbuckle—1955
W. H. Rivers, III—1956-57
Jesse C. Miller—1958
Albert Mikulencak—1959
H. L. Neidig—1960
Ray Arbuckle, Jr.—1961
Bill R. Black—1962
Joe Simon—1963
Guy Carter—1964
Lawson Rivers—1965
Eugene Pruess—1966
Homer H. Newby—1967
Alvin Langhamer—1968
Charley C. Smith—1969-70
James Witschorke—1971-72

The organization sponsors special community projects, the special project for 1972 being Elgin's Centennial Celebration.

XIII ENTERTAINMENT

Extra hours spent frying chicken over hot stoves, pains taken in chopping pecans to sprinkle over the icing on a three-layered cake, and the care exercised in ironing ruffles on white dresses were forgotten by early Elgin residents once they reached the picnic site. Yet, many of the older citizens today recall those picnics and barbecues as outstanding moments of yesteryear.

Only the real oldtimers remember the Town and Country Picnic of August 2, 1900. Under the oak grove approximately one half mile east of Elgin, where the present Woodlawn Addition is, they spread their picnic baskets, after which Congressman Albert Sydney Burleson delivered an oration. Burleson later would accept an appointment as postmaster general of the U.S.

In the audience was James Stephen Hogg, who had been the first native Texan to occupy the governor's chair. When he wasn't listening to Burleson, Gov. Hogg mingled with Elginites, promoting William Jennings Bryan as presidential material. Also in the crowd were all county officers.

"Stirring music vied with the oratory of the big politicians," remembers one person who was present at the picnic. The New Sweden Band was the source of the music. Musicians had been hired to play all day, and they kept the oak grove filled with stirring sounds.

Watermelons were ripe, and citizens were filled with patriotism on July 4, 1908, when a large picnic and barbecue was held on the hill where the homes of the late W. H. Rivers Jr. and E. Roy Jones are today. Each family brought baskets and boxes of homemade food, but Mrs. Homer T. Ward, Sr., gave Elgin citizens something to talk about when she unloaded a round-topped trunk filled with delicacies from her kitchen.

When talk about Mrs. Ward's picnic container died, a green grape pie eating contest was held.

And once again Elginites, groaning from filled stomachs, listened to music. This time the marches, waltzes, and polkas came from the trumpets and trombones of Round Rock musicians, whose leader was dressed in a white uniform. One young boy, awed by the appearance of the conductor, tugged at his mother's fluffy white dress. When the mother failed to pay attention, the youngster hollered, "Look, Ma, he has on his long underwear!"

Elgin residents observed July 4, 1919, by assembling at Carter's Park, located on Burleson Creek approximately one mile from Elgin on the Pleasant Grove Road. Red, white and blue bunting was sensitive to any whiff of breeze, as candidates for county office related campaign promises.

Excitement of the political rally was matched by the enthusiasm of baseball games and by the frenzy of horse racing, the type done in today's Western Pleasure Shows in which the jockey, using a javelin, gathers rings from a series of posts.

By nightfall, the speakers' stand bunting sagged, picnic baskets were empty, ice cream freezers were ringed with salty water, race horses were blanketed, frilly white dresses drooped, and celluloid collars were smudged, but memories were bright and Elgin had another page in her book of history.

* * * *

By 1892, a ribbon of large opera houses spanned Texas, from Galveston and Houston to San Antonio and Austin to Fort Worth and Dallas, each house capable of accommodating a thousand patrons. These opera houses offered physical facilities that leading dramatists required for their traveling troupes. A number of less commodious houses were erected in smaller communities throughout the state, and rising stars, political hopefuls, and young singers found their boards ideal nurseries for their talents.

Elgin had two opera houses. The first was located in the Standifer Building, corner of Depot Street and North Main. On its stage appeared singers, instrumentalists, bands, lecturers, and thespians. The second theatre, Bassist Opera House located on the west corner of South Avenue C and Central Street, provided Elgin men and women with the opportunity not only to be entertained and to become cultured but also with the chance to "dress up." Aware of the fashion of wearing large hats festonned with maline and egert and ostrich plumes, the manager of the Bassist once posted this notice:

"If the ladies want the whole population to rise up and bless them, they will go to the Opera House tonight with small hats, or none at all. Do not defraud your neighbor, but give him a chance to see the show."

On another occasion, women were promised a photograph of Little Lord Fauntleroy, who was "playing at the Opera House" Thursday night.

The Opera Houses also fostered local talent, providing the stage for dance, piano, and instrumental recitals. On the boards too were staged charity benefits.

Elgin's interest in culture was manifest in other ways. Upon learning about the Chautauqua movement, a New York state-based operation responsible for sending out speakers, musiicans, and troupes of performers, a group of Elgin residents checked into the possibility of getting their hometown on the circuit of educational and cultural programs. By 1900, approximately 400 communities, among them Elgin, were included on the Chautauqua trail. When Chautauqua artists appeared in Elgin, they frequently performed under a tent, usually set up on a vacant lot near the old water tower, on the corner of Lexington Road and North Main.

To early Elginites the erection of a tent must have been synonymous with excitement, for the Chautauqua events were not the only ones which unfolded under canvas. Each year, old and young alike looked forward to the coming of the circus, the carnival, the Wild West show, and the Tent Shows.

Among the first of the circus groups to delight Elgin audiences was the Gentry Brothers Dog and Pony Show, the troupe of which usually arrived by train. Gathered to witness the unloading were crowds of children and adults. Young boys of the town vied with each other for the free passes rewarded those who watered the elephants; they soon learned that it took a lot of water to fill an elephant, however!

One of the earliest Wild West shows to come to town was one called "Booger Red," which had no tent but held performances on the old baseball park near the present Methodist Latin American Mission. The Buffalo Bill Shows brought "live" Indians to Elgin. The manager of the show once claimed to have Geronimo in his troupe, and the newspaper in 1886, had this to say about the warrior chief.

"Geronimo was a most delapidated specimen—his hair was long and was hanging over his dirty shoulders in a reckless manner. He was dressed in a dingy suit, looking more like a squaw than a murderous chief. He was also sullen and refused to talk."

Elgin residents looked forward each year to the arrival of the Hardley Sadler Tent Show, the troupe of which remained in town a week, producing a different show each night. The villians in these melodramas performed so effectively they pulled tears from many women in the audience.

One of the chief attractions at carnivals was the baloon ascension. The balloon, filled with hot air, usually rose to 500 or 1,000 feet, then drifted with the wind, and landed several miles from town, depending on the wind velocity. The balloon usually pulled a basket in which a man rode, but on one occasion a monkey substituted for the man. Children clapped their hands and squealed with delight as the monkey became airborne.

Medicine show wagons frequently arrived in town, taking a central location to entertain Elginites with singing, dancing, comedy skits, and clever but tricky salesmanship. One wagon arrived bearing this sign: "KKK—Ku Klux Klan—often carries terror to the hearts of many, but K.K.K.—Kay's Kentucky Kure—is the only liniment that brings peace to the hearts of those who use it." The sign on another medicine show wagon promoted Frehgh's Remedy, "a medicine that will very rapidly and effectually remove the cause of rheumatism, neuralgia, and gout from the system."

These shows drew crowds, and by the time of the night performance, the town was filled with buggies and wagons. And when the wagons of performers pulled out, bottles of liniment were left behind. Results? Miraculous cures? Memories fail to recall.

* * * *

Band concerts, like the traveling medicine shows, pulled hundreds of persons to town, and a band stand in the center of City Park accommodated the musical groups that serenaded Elgin residents.

On the prairie north of Elgin, the musically inclined Swedish people early had their neighborhood bands. New Sweden, Lund and Carlson communities had bands around the turn of the century. About 1910, Elgin had a band with J. B. Clopton, an optometrist, as its leader. Clopton also made violins of such excellence that they were in great demand. The musicians met to practice in his home which was located on the site of the Medical-Dental Clinic. This band functioned until the beginning of World War I, playing at public gatherings, marching in parades and providing community entertainment.

Many of the musicians that played with the Elgin band and those from the Swedish communities later played in the American Legion Band, whose directors through the years were Otto Wolf, Theo Thornquist, Martin Lind, and Will Nichols. For years, this band was a regular participant in Fourth of July picnics, political speakings, and other public gatherings. Concerts in the band stand in the City Park were a delight during the summer months.

* * * *

Athletics have also filled leisure moments for area residents. A newspaper in the late 1800s commented that croquet was a popular form of entertainment, one appealing to all members of the family. Croquet, the reporter indicated, was a "very fashionable game, particularly among the young ladies and gentlemen."

Throughout the years, baseball has held a place in the hearts of residents. On December 16, 1887, the Texas League was born in Austin, and players and fans alike took a renewed interest in the sport. And, throughout the years, Elgin has fielded winning teams, but the 1907 squad probably heads the list. Members of the team included Charlie Carter, Pat Burns, Hinds Carter, Mann Outlaw, Charles E. Davis, Max and Charles Holchac, Hal Meeks, Virgil King, Charlie Wilkes, and Dan McCullough, manager.

"Elgin Blues"—year 1907. Back row: Hinds Carter, Pat Burns, Charlie Carter, Mann Outlaw, Ed Davis. Second row: Charlie Holchak, Don McCullough, Hal Meeks, Max Holchak. Sitting, Virgil King and Charlie Wilkes.

Henry A. Lundgren American Legion Band in 1928.

Charlie Carter, who later took the mound for Galveston in the Texas League, was once described as "one of the best pitchers in Texas."

Jim Keeble's miniature golf course was the scene of happy times for thousands. Located on North Main, where the Gruetzner used car lot is, the course provided family entertainment and staged tournaments for children and adults.

Leon Rivers and associates built a golf course on the Sayersville Road and Elginites had a new form of entertainment. Club fees were paid, and members were permitted to enjoy the sand greens. Later George Prewitt established a nine-hole golf course on the Elgin Standard Brick Co. property, and the operation became known as Elgin Country Club. The course had a club house and grass greens, and was the scene of a number of tournaments. Also connected with the course was a baseball field with brick grandstands, where matched games were played.

* * * *

About 1906, Elginites began going in circles, for that year a skating rink was built on South Main, below the site of the Davis and Schanhals garage. In operating the rink, W. C. Brown and Brooks Carter provided a chance for Elgin residents to gain exercise or to be spectators; they also provided a building in which union revivals and graduation exercises were staged.

* * * *

Sometime before 1908, Elgin's first movie house, the Majestic Theater, opened where a metal building now stands west of Davis and Schanhals Pontiac Co. Ikey Tindler was owner, and his first projectionist, Joe Sandgarten, hand cranked the Edison Kinetoscope projector. Tindler used a gasoline engine-driven direct-current dynamo for his electricity.

The front of the theater was illuminated by a row of colored electric light bulbs, a wonder to Elginites at the time. After each nightly performance, Tindler would step before the screen to announce, "same thing tomorrow night, only different."

Admission was 5 and 10 cents.

In 1909 Tindler moved the theater to the location of Dorleen's dress shop on North Main, and later in the year it was sold to E. W. Nichols and P. Torno. Occasionally, stage events were added to the programs.

In 1910 the Enterprise Theater opened its doors on the location of Ramsey's Drug Store. Several times over the years the theater changed owners.

In 1913, the IMP Theater put up its marquee in the area where Margaret's Beauty Shop is on Depot Street. The theater took its name from "Independent Motion Pictures" and was an open air theater at first. Only the front part, that which housed the ticket office and the projection booth, had a roof. Business, therefore, was good only so long as the weather was good.

Each night Buster Clark, representing the IMP Theater, and John Nichols, representing the Enterprise Theater, barked their programs up and down Main Street. Each used a long megaphone so that he could be heard away in the residential section.

The Enterprise closed its doors after a few years, but it was 1930 before the IMP went out of business. The IMP had moved several times, its last location being the site of the drive-in section of Elgin National Bank. In June, 1930, Dale Willson bought it and made major improvements and changed the name to Elgin Theater. About 1942, Willson opened the present Eltex Theater.

Special train bound for Landa Park in New Braunfels in 1909, where Elginites annually made excursions for picnics. This was a complimentary special honoring W. H. Rivers, President, Texas State Bankers Association.

XIV JUST REMINISCING

In 1870, the average wage in Bastrop County was $15 a month. Milk cows sold for $10, stock cows for $5, and sheep for $1 each.

Bastrop County's population in 1870 was 12,290 and 1,258 of these were foreign born.

An early writer said that the first wedding in Elgin was that of Sarah E. Gordon and E. D. Durfee on November 21, 1873.

On the Bahn farm, located 5 miles south of Elgin, there was an oil well prior to the discovery of Spindle Top, near Beaumont. While digging a water well in 1891, Mr. Bahn found oil at 338 feet. Though it was not in commercial quantities, it was used through the years for fuel and to lubricate farm equipment.

Wilhelm Bahn house built in 1887 by itinerant German rock mason from rock hauled by ox teams more than 25 miles. A frame house now stands on this location.

In 1906 Jake Hanson and Son advertised that Elgin's first bottling works was ready and that he would "supply the very best bottled soda water that can be made."

From an April, 1908, *Courier* we read, "Mr. C. B. Caffey of the Elgin Fruit Farms states that the berry crop this year will be enormous. He expects to begin shipping in a few days and expects to continue for some time."

Wagon displaying products of the J. B. Morrison Bakery in a 1905 parade, with Willie Wilson, the baker, as the driver.

The August 15, 1908, *Courier* said, "Last Saturday was one of those old time, long to be remembered, old-fashioned Saturdays in Elgin. They were here from the forks of the creek, the head waters down in the oaks, from out in the mesquites, from among the prickly pears, and from off the prairies. The fall rush is on. Hundreds of pickers have come in, and wagon after wagon load of provisions could be seen leaving town."

Elgin's first celebration of the Mexican Independence was observed on September 16, 1908 with a three day celebration. A big dance was held in the skating rink which was decorated with Mexican flags. On the 16th, there was a parade with Miss Jesusita Enriques portraying the Queen of Montezumas, and Miss Andrea Garcia as the American Goddess of Liberty. The celebration was a big success.

Mexican Independence Day celebration on September 16, 1923. U. Santos served as chairman and Joe Pena served as secretary of the twenty member committee of arrangements.

The Dr. T. B. Taylor house, as it moved up Main Street in front of early day homes of J. F. Meeks and R. V. Standifer—now the 200 block of North Main.

It is nothing for a house to be moved in our modern times, but none can equal the story of Dr. T. B. Taylor's large two-story house. In the early 1900's Dr. Taylor moved to Elgin from Paige, where the house was originally built. It was torn down and moved to Elgin to the lot where the Wallace Gillum home (originally built by J. C. Miller, Sr.) now stands. In 1908 Dr. Taylor bought several lots in the Wade and Owens addition and moved his big house to its location, about where the R. H. Arbuckle, Sr. home is now situated. The project took over a month, and was done by using a winch hooked to a post in the middle of the street. The family lived in the house while it was in transit to its new location. After several years in this location the stately house was destined for another move. This time it was torn down and reconstructed almost in its original architecture in Bastrop when Dr. Taylor left Elgin to practice medicine there. The house still exists today as a residence.

Train with nine flat cars loaded with Elgin cotton in 1908; Joe King and Max Hirsch, standing by the train.

In 1909 nearly 13,000 bales of cotton were marketed in Elgin. A first in the town's history took place in December of that year. Mr. N. P. Lundgren brought a bale of cotton to town on a sleigh, as there had been a big sleet storm. The bale was purchased by W. E .McCullough at 14½¢ a pound.

In 1910, the *Elgin Courier* carried the following story: "My friend, did you know that we have enough clay around this town to wall this old state in from the world. We have 4 of the finest brick plants in Texas right in our doors and hardly a town in Texas that hasn't a building made of them. We predict that Elgin can easily become the center of brick manufacturing for the entire southwest with a little publicity."

A 1910 writer said that he did not know that Elgin had so many automobiles until the previous Sunday when they were all out with families enjoying the evening.

The culmination of a struggle of several years saw the establishment of Elgin's downtown city park in late 1912 when the ladies of the Civic Improvement Committee signed a lease with the railroad for the right-of-way land which had been occupied by a lumber yard. After securing a place to re-locate Mutual Lumber Company, a new building was built by them on the McGinnis property (now Mogonye Lumber Company) and they completed their move there in October 1912. The railroad assisted the ladies in their plans for the park, and early in 1913, plans began shaping up for sidewalks, setting

Cars lined up for the parade down Main Street, in 1910, present location of Main and First Street.

Bandstand, in the City Park, where band concerts held were a delight during the summer months.

of trees, shrubs and flowers. A bandstand was built, and the park soon blossomed into a real beauty spot, becoming a gathering place for many city functions and public entertainment.

An early Elgin playground became famous as a beauty spot and gathering place when Oscar Bones cleared a site north of Elgin (near the old North School and adjoining the Wilson property at that time). Sometime in 1912, Bones began clearing the land, trimming trees and ridding the area of prickly pears and brush. By the spring of 1913, the area was covered with lush grass; benches, swings and see-saws had been added, as well as a band stand. Sunday afternoon found large crowds gathered for the activities there and enjoying the natural beauty of the outdoors.

Nursing baby rattle snakes proved profitable to an Elgin youth in 1915. Young Roy (Dutch) Frazier was feeding hundreds of snakes on the Wade Ranch which was two miles north of town. The hissing of the snakes, which corresponded to the crowing of the chickens in the morning, could be heard by early risers for hundreds of yards from the ranch. Frazier kept them in pens and fed them meat. It proved a lucrative endeavor, for he was offered 25¢ a pound for all snakes he could bring in, to be used to make snake oil for medicinal purposes.

Elgin is not only well known for its brick making, but also for its hot sausage. People come from far and wide to eat it. It has been known for a helicopter to land on the side of the freight depot in order for someone to get several pounds to take back to Austin for lunch for some office workers. When the Lyndon B. Johnson Library was dedicated in Austin, various dignitaries and newsmen came from Washington for the event. When the chartered plane for the newsmen was ready to depart for its return trip, a gentleman, who barely made it in time for the take off, got on the plane carrying a box containing 40 pounds of Elgin hot sausage.

In 1922, a charity organization, called the Elgin Blue Cross, was organized to help those in need among the Mexican population. Dances, suppers, and various other means were used to raise money to support the organization. Many people were helped by its members.

Mr. Jake Mecey in 1922 put in Elgin's first beauty shop in connection with his "Queen's Shop", ladies ready-to-wear- on the Southside.

Mrs. W. H. (Lula) Standifer in 1923 operated a beauty shop in her home. For about a year she took her equipment to Giddings two days a week, in her car, to take care of her customers there. From then on for several decades she did the beauty work for the women

Little folks enjoying themselves on see-saws at the playground.

Southside Meat Market where Elgin's famous hot sausage was first made. From left to right behind the meat counter; Bud Frazier, Leo Maass, and Lee Wilson, owner.

of Elgin and its environs. Many of her first permanents were given with the spiral machine; later she used the croquonol method.

John Puckett built his first radio and obtained a HAM radio license in 1923. By request, he would broadcast phonograph music. One of his first requests was from a lady in Bartlett. She was entertaining the Ladies Aid Society on Thursday afternoon and asked him to broadcast during that hour. This gave him a great deal of pleasure.

Miller Radio Shop in Elgin in the summer of 1933 sponsored the El-Tex Radio Station, operated by Mr. Ned Miller, called "Uncle Ned", who put on local talent skits, songs and entertainment to the delight of the 30 or 40 kiddies who participated each Saturday. Nell Puckett was the director and Margaret McCullough the accompanist. Sunday morning broadcasts included services at the Methodist Church.

In 1937 a young man came to town campaigning for the office of Representative of the Tenth District in Congress. His coming to speak had been advertised, and Elgin citizens were standing on both sides of Main Street for about two blocks. Mrs. C. W. Webb had been chosen to introduce him, and her introduction included the following words: "This personable young man, Lyndon B. Johnson, who in so short a time has accomplished so very much—both in Washington, as an able assistant in the office of Congressman Kleberg, and in Texas as the dynamic, ingenious power in the N.Y.A. office—will shortly, by his proven abilities in the House of Representatives to which this District will send him, be recognized as the *Leader* of our United States; and, before long, we'll be proud to welcome him as the nation's President in the White House." There may have been others who recognized the unusual ability of Mr. Johnson, but it is probable that Mrs. Webb was the first to predict publicly that he would some day become President of the United States.

In July 1941, came the word from Congressman Lyndon B. Johnson that Uncle Sam was to build a new army camp in Bastrop County, but then in September it was announced that it was probable that the army would not expand. Then came Pearl Harbor! Fifty-two thousand acres of land were bought between Elgin and Bastrop, and the people living there were forced to move off. All of the towns in the area were filled with construction workers, and every available room in Elgin was rented to workers. By the summer of 1942 Camp Swift was almost completed. Committees were appointed to help Elgin handle the increase in population. Servicemen brought their wives, and they lived in every available apartment and room that could be made livable. Camp Swift provided employment for hundred's of Elgin's citizens. Rationing had gone into effect on the home front. Gasoline, tires, and shoes were rationed, as well as sugar, coffee, canned and processed foods, meats, edible fats and oils, cheese and canned fish. No Yule lights brightened the

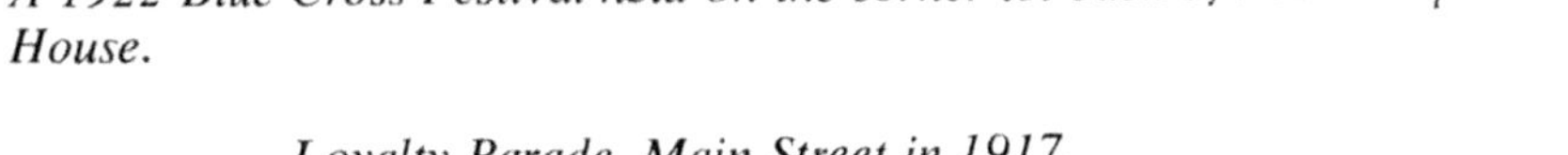

A 1922 Blue Cross Festival held on the corner lot back of Bassist Opera House.

Loyalty Parade, Main Street in 1917.

streets at Christmas time as the War Department had requested that critical resources be conserved. Elgin's sons and daughters served in all branches of the service, some giving their lives for their country. It was a time of joy and thanksgiving when peace came and families were reunited.

During Camp Swift days, from 1942 to 1945, there was a Bastrop County Camp-Hospital Council in which all organizations in the county participated. Each organization from the various towns took turns in providing weekly delicacies of homemade ice cream and cakes for the patients in the different hospital wards in Camp Swift.

In 1940—Elgin at its nearby Elgin Standard Brick Company had an Airport available with a 3-way landing field. Prior to then Geo. K. (Buddy) Prewitt had a private landing field located at Elgin Standard's Park, now part of Elgin Butler Brick Plant.

The first Mid-Summer Swedish Festival held in Elgin was in June, 1946. Annually, hundreds of people are in attendance at the banquet and special program given.

September, 1954, Main Street was solidly lined on both sides with people, waiting to witness the big parade of Elgin's Fifth Yamboree. Elgin has long been known for its good yams, and this year for the best yams the first prize was awarded to Tallie Pate and second place to Dale Carter.

On December 20, 1955, and December 21, 1965, the New Century Club staged most unusual Christmas pageants, with Mrs. Wayne Davenport serving as president of the club and Mrs. Paul Farris as chairman of the pageant committee. Through the co-operation of all churches of the town, the Story of Christ was depicted on floats which moved along Main Street. Each church provided a float, with the characters in costume, depicting their particular part of the story. Church choirs provided the musical background for each portrayal. Following the downtown parade, the program was concluded at the High School football field, where special program numbers were given.

After World War II Elgin experienced a steady growth in its residential and business districts, and its population increased through the years as follows:

1940—2,008
1950—3,168
1960—3,511
1970—3,832

Recreational facilities consist of a well-kept 17 acre Elgin Memorial Park, with baseball, Little League, tennis courts, play and picnic areas. It is here that the Elgin Centennial Marker, 1872-1972, will be placed.

Cars lined up for Elgin's First Trade Excursion, on lot where William's Grocery is now being built.

Elgin's Main Street back in 1916.

Elgin's Main Street, looking North, in the early 1920's.

Main Street in the late 1940's.

XV ELGIN TODAY 1972

When the officials of the Houston and Texas Central Railroad Company on August 18, 1872, executed their Deed of Dedication for the town that they officially named "Elgin", they set in motion activities that helped develop an area that has gained renown, not only for its agricultural and industrial accomplishments, but for men and women whose influence for good has continued.

To this area came early enterprising business people and settlers who established a culture greatly influenced by six ethnic groups, composed of Anglo-American, Negro, German, Mexican, Swedish and Czech; and all, through concerted action, brought about the growth of present day Elgin, the largest city in Bastrop County, with a population of 3,832.

Today, one hundred years since its founding, Elgin can be proud of its growth, its thriving businesses, its good schools, its many churches, its fine homes, and its people who live as good neighbors and bid welcome to all who come into their midst.

In the preceding accounts, we wish that in some way we could have more completely told of the remarkable qualities of vision, faith, and determination of the people who through the past century have moulded this community. We can look back with pride and into the future with hope, that those who will mould it for the next century will continue to preserve the great heritage that is ours, so that Elgin will always be the finest town we know in which to live.

The compilers of this book express gratitude to all who helped make, and are making, the Elgin of today, and cordially salute all those who will take their places in 2072, one hundred years hence.

Main Street, Elgin today, 1972.

Elgin Today ... 2002
THE NEXT 100 YEARS

The unprecedented interest in Elgin, Bastrop County, Texas, has brought about change in many different ways. A brief highlight of the additions to Elgin follow:

The Elgin/Fleming Hospital closed in 1983, but at the former site is now Morris Memorial Park (for Dr. Roy Morris) and Elgin's first public swimming pool, which opened in 1995.

Highway 290 to Austin is now a four-lane, divided highway.

Elgin's City Hall is now located in the historical Nofsinger House in downtown Elgin, on Main Street.

In 1990, Elgin became a Main Street City, a downtown revitalization and beautification program of the Texas Historical Association. In 2002, Elgin's current Main Street director is Amy Miller. The downtown area is designated as an Historical District, and it is listed on the National Register.

The new Elgin High School opened in 2001 on the west side of Elgin in Travis County, formerly farmland for cotton, corn, wheat and milo.

The area of Elgin known as "the south side" of downtown is currently being restored after years of neglect, and old and new business and residential inhabitants are reaping the rewards with visitors and charm.

The oldest building in Elgin, the old freight depot on the north side of the east-west railroad track downtown, is now restored and houses a Visitor's Center and the Elgin Chamber of Commerce, just a few feet from Veterans Memorial Park with restored grounds and a gazebo.

The 1903 Union Depot has now been restored at a general cost of $500 thousand dollars and is the home of Elgin's first museum.

A Texas grocery tradition, H.E.B., opened in Elgin in 2001 on Highway 290.

Major housing subdivisions started popping up on the black dirt "prairie" west of Elgin in 2001.

A new public library building begins construction in 2002. The first meeting of the Elgin Library Board met in 1986. The formation of the library board was a 1986 Texas Sesquicentennial Committee project for the community by co-chairmen Sandy Murphree and Betty Lynn Meyer.

And...we now have a red light on Main Street. Also, three stop lights on Highway 290 and one on Highway 95 North. Wow!

ELGIN, for many years, has been known as a "Community of Churches". There is no measure by which to determine the continuing and upbuilding influence of such on the life of our people! In an attempt to acknowledge their worth, we are presenting in this historic publication a list of the names of the present congregations; their current ministers; and the numerical enrollment of each. Emma S. Webb, Jackson S. Webb, Ross Meredith.

* * * *

1874 Elgin Methodist, Rev. Bob Blackwell 362
1875 Elgin First Baptist, Rev. Ray Head 738
1876 New Sweden Lutheran, Rev. Ernest Messer 135
1881 Elgin Presbyterian, Rev. W. F. Galbraith 67
1888 Central Christian, Rev. Carroll Weedon 85
1888 Mt. Pleasant Missionary Baptist, Rev. Matthew Carter 75
(At Piney Creek first; Elgin 1946)
1889 Mt. Moriah Missionary Baptist, Rev. R. A. Westbrook 150
(Had Pleasant Grove group 1879; present site 1889)
1892 Manda Methodist (combined with Elgin Meth. 1962)
1897 Lund Lutheran, Rev. Ernest Messer 115
1897 Kimbro Evangelical Free (combined with Elgin Free 1954)
1898 Mt. Vernon A.M.E., Rev. Julia Francis 47
1905 Pleasant Bethany Baptist, Rev. J. E. James 209
1908 Sacred Heart Catholic, Rev. Everett Trebtoske 900
1908 Type Evangelical Free (combined with Elgin Free 1954)
1909 Seventh-Day Adventist, Pastor Jim Tucker 68
(A. J. Jensen home; PeLee 1912; Elgin 1951)
1910 German Baptist (combined with Elgin First Baptist 1949)
1911 Elgin Church of Christ, Minister Gaston Welborn 100
1917 Elgin Assembly of God, Rev. E. L. Carter 25
1918 St. Peters Evangelical Lutheran, Rev. Jas. Witschorche 372
1924 Bethel Methodist (1956), Rev. Marta Rye 59
(originally Methodist Mexican Mission)
1933 Winn Memorial Baptist, Rev. J. R. Williams 104
1936 Lakeview Baptist, Rev. Lee Collins 40
1950 Church of God in Christ (Holiness), Rev. Morris Williams 12
1951 Baptist Mexican Mission, Mr. Faustino Armendariz
(Branch of Elgin First Baptist)
1952 Mt. Carmel Missionary Baptist, Rev. Q. C. Goins 90
1952 East Side Church of Christ (Combined with Elgin Church 1970)
1953 Church of God (Pentecostal), Rev. Joy Matthews 35
1954 Elgin Evangelical Free, Rev. Kenneth Bergstedt 70
1956 Grace Lutheran, Rev. Robt. L. Hartfield 110
1956 Immanuel Seventh-Day Adventist, Pastor Artis Wagner 25
1957 Mt. Olive Assembly of God, Rev. Alicia Cantu 12
1970 Elgin First Christian, Rev. Richard D. Robison 53

ERROTA

(Addition, Page 1, third paragraph) Mary Buchanan Christian Burleson was from Virginia. Her parents were friends of Thomas Jefferson. She knew Moses and Stephen Austin. She met Thomas Christian while visiting cousins in Kentucky. She was 32 when she and Thomas Christian moved to Texas. They built the fifth log cabin in Bastrop County. Mr. Christian was killed by Comanches in the attack when Josiah Wilbarger was scalped. She then married Captain James Burleson. He and his son were in the Alamo at the Siege of Bexar. After his death, his son, Edward Burleson, was second in command at Battle of San Jacinto and is first person buried in the State Cemetery in Austin. After the Runaway Scrape, she briefly fled to Fort Parker in Limestone County, named for founders Silas M. and brother, James W. Parker. Silas was the father of Cynthia Ann Parker, who was kidnapped by Comanches in 1836 along with four other family members.

As these things were told by Clyde Reynolds of Bastrop and Dr. Bryon L. Howard in 1999, they said there were still organized buffalo hunts around this area in 1839. The Christian colony, or land grant, was the outermost colony at that time. And there were Indians around here for the next 30 years.

(Addition, Page 4) re: By 1885, there were eight passenger trains passing through Elgin a day. Elgin was a tough and rowdy town.It was a typical western town. There were seven saloons about one for every 16 adult males. The town attracted gamblers and prostitutes. It got so bad that the railroad conductors, when announcing Elgin often yelled, "Hell-gin, half Way to Hades, next stop". The Bigger Inn was the site of one of these saloons. In 1897, Mr. A.S. Christian, a descendant of Mary Christian Burleson, bought the lot for $300. and built the present structure. It has been used for a bus station, bottling plant, and other commercial uses from its saloon days to the 1970s and then was vacant for about 20 years Restoration was started by James Biggers, and after his death, completed by his sister, Dorothy Biggers Cartwright in the 1990s. There was a large sign painted on the side of the building which read, "A. Christian Saloon" to attract customers. The story is that a Bible salesman who got off the train, saw the sign and was impressed with the idea of a Christian saloon. He rushed into the saloon to congratulate the owner, but made a hasty retreat after learning that the establishment was not as he had thought!

(Addition, Page 6) re: John Litton came as immigrant from Missouri, died Bastrop Co. on April 4, 1856. Born in North Carolina in 1810, was in Captain Jesse Billingsley Co. in Texas War of Independence. Then was with ranging company under Captain John McGehee in Burleson's Regiment; was in several Indian skirmishes, including Plum Creek in 1842; was owner of Litton Inn, a stage stand in Perryville; also first postmaster of Young's Settlement and Perryville; his wife, Sarah Standifer Litton, died February 9, 1892.

(Addition, Page 10) re: Elginites awaiting President McKinley's train in May 1901. Noel Branton of Elgin told Donald Whitten that his mother had heard on the party line that the president was coming to town but he was down on the creek picking dewberries.

(Addition, Page 31) Armando Olvera, January 31, 1976.

(Addition, Page 91 fourth paragraph) Unfortunately, Fleming Memorial Hospital closed in 1983 due to low occupancy and financial troubles. Two hospital benefits (1978 & 1982) kept it going awhile longer. Lady Bird Johnson and Liz Carpenter headlined the 1978 benefit, a chili supper for 900 at the Elgin SPJST Hall.

(Addition, Page 123) Lyndon B. Johnson came to Elgin on April 7, 1937. The election was on April 10. After leaving Elgin that day, he proceeded to visit Paige, McDade, Bastrop and Smithville.

(Addition, Page 125) Elgin's first Yamboree was held in 1949.

(Addition, Page 125) Elgin's early populations included: 1872 (250); 1890 (831); 1900 (1,258).

(Addition, Page 12) The Eltex Theater closed in 1984. It occupied the site of the present Elgin Bank of Texas drop box on Main Street, then later moved slightly south to the parking lot owned by Elgin Bank, next to City Café.

(Correction, Page 26) Second paragraph: dial (dail).

(Addition, Page 135) Elgin Cotton Oil Mill, founded 1904.

(Addition, Page 141) Elgin Courier, founded 1890.

(Addition, Page 144) Elgin Insurance Agency, founded 1957, by Weldon Whitten.

(Correction, Page 152) prosper (proper).

(Addition, Page 153) Meyer's Sausage Co., founded 1949.

(Addition, Page 154) Margaret's Beauty Shop, founded 1932.

(Addition, Page 154) South Side Market and Bar-B-Que, founded 1892.

THE ELGIN NATIONAL BANK

31 North Main

Phone 285-3913

The original bank, The Bank of Elgin, was begun in 1891, and was privately owned by W. H. (Bud) Rivers. It was located in the Rivers and Carter brick store on South Side.

On April 21, 1906, the bank was incorporated as The Elgin National Bank. President was W. H. Rivers, Cashier was James Keeble, and W. H. Rivers, Jr. was Assistant Cashier. Directors were W. H. Rivers, James Keeble, A. H. Carter, J. C. Orgain, W. P. Culp, P. C. Wells, and I. B. Nofsinger, M.D.

In the summer of 1909, the founder, Mr. W. H. Rivers, died. W. H. Rivers, Jr. then served as President. In 1923, the bank moved to its present location on Main Street.

Following the death of W. H. Rivers, Jr., in 1960, R. H. Arbuckle, Sr. was appointed President. Mr. Arbuckle served until January, 1961, when W. H. Rivers, III was elected President. Mr. W. H. Rivers, III served in that capacity until his sudden death in June, 1971.

At the beginning of 1972, Mr. Lawson Rivers was appointed President, with Ray Arbuckle, Jr. serving as Executive Vice-President. Etta Mae Carter is Cashier and Kenneth Danklefs is Assistant Cashier. Beginning the year as Directors were R. H. Arbuckle, Sr., Chairman of the Board, Mrs. Betty Rivers, Mrs. Elizabeth Rivers Caudill, W. C. Rivers, Jr., J. K. Prewitt, W. H. Cardwell, D.V.M., Roy Morris M.D., E. O. Lundgren, Jr., and the President and Executive Vice-President already named.

The bank is proud to have been instrumental in the growth and development of Elgin in the past century, and we assure you that we will utilize the foresight and faith of our heritage to help Elgin grow into an even better community in the future.

Member FDIC

O'CONNOR FURNITURE

Quality Home Furnishings Since 1892

Elgin's oldest retail business firm, owned and operated by three generations of the O'Connor family.

Thomas O'Connor—1892-1919

Edgar O'Connor—1919-1953

Joseph O'Connor—1953 to present

As Elgin begins its second century, we re-dedicate ourselves to you, our customer.

ELGIN FARMER'S UNION WAREHOUSE COMPANY

P. O. Box 589

Phone 285-4836

This business was organized September 15, 1906, with the following officers and directors: William McWilliams, President; H. Bahn, Secretary-Treasurer; and Directors, E. H. Goyne, W. C. Rankin, H. Bahn, Alf Anderson, and Gus O. Seaholm. The company organized and built a warehouse for receiving, storing, and shipping cotton. The business has been in operation for 66 years. Present officers of the union are Lawson Rivers, President and Treasurer; W. L. Rivers, Vice-President; and David Swenson, Secretary. The Directors are E. O. Lundgren, Jr., Ralph Lundgren, Wesley Frederickson, C. T. Larsberg, and Arthur Schroeder, Jr. The manager is George Loftus.

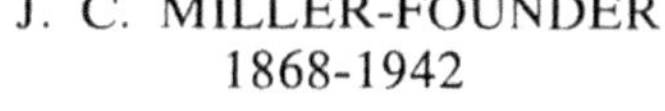

J. C. MILLER-FOUNDER
1868-1942

In 1903 J. C. Miller purchased a furniture and funeral business from Leon and Walter Keeble. The business, known as J. C. Miller Furniture, was located on South Avenue C. In 1905, the J. C. Miller Furniture Company moved to 22 North Main Street. In 1913, the firm moved into a newly constructed building at 117-119 North Main Street. In 1927, the 117 North Main Street location was converted into a Funeral Chapel. A modern funeral home, Miller Mortuary, was built in 1941 at 209 North Avenue C. Mr. J. C. Miller died in August, 1942, and his two sons, Jesse and Cecil R. Miller, continued to operate the business until 1965, when Miller Mortuary was sold to Homer H. Newby. The mortuary was then known as the Miller-Newby Funeral Home. The two brothers, Jesse and Cecil, operated the Miller Furniture Company until 1972, Elgin's Centennial Year, when the business was sold, in February, to Robert E. Barker. The business is now known as Barker Home Furnishings.

J. C. MILLER FURNITURE COMPANY

1903-1972

MILLER MORTUARY

1903-1965

BARKER HOME FURNISHING

117 North Main

Phone 285-3559

Originally Miller Furniture Company, which was established in 1903, Barker Home Furnishings offers the home owner everything in complete home furnishings.

Bob Barker, owner and manager, has been an Elgin resident for five years. He is married to the former Karin Lundgren, and they have two children, Barry and Kara.

For the young set, Barker Home Furnishings features bassinets, high chairs, and baby beds. They have complete furnishings for living room, dining room, bed room, and kitchen. In appliances, they carry Maytag washers and dryers, refrigerators by Frigidaire, and a large variety of small appliances by Sunbeam and Hoover. A new addition Mr. Barker has added for the people of Elgin is a complete line of Dan River Carpet and Majestic pre-fab fireplaces, either traditional or contemporary. If you enjoy watching TV or listening to beautiful music, let Bob show you a Zenith or RCA television, stereo, or radio.

Drop by and see Bob on the corner at 117 North Main Street and keep Barker Home Furnishings in mind for all of your home furnishings needs.

RAY'S BARBER SHOP

Mr. Roy Ray set up his barber practice in 1910 in the shop that now is Dor-Leen's Ladies' Dress Shop. A year later he moved across Main Street to the present location at Mikulencak's. His brother, D. B. Ray, joined him in 1920. In 1940, the business was relocated at its present location, 113 North Main. Mr. Ray passed away in 1971, after barbering for 61 years. Mr. Ray's estate still owns the shop, which is now run by his brother, D. B. Mrs. Roy Ray and the late Mr. Ray have two sons, Curtis of Elgin, and Lynn of Lubbock. In 1934, the Rays were blessed with their first grandson, Jon Lynn. Jonnie, as he was affectionately called, and Mr. Ray had a special bond that lasted throughout their lives. Jonnie died eight months after his grandfather in November, 1971. There are six other grandchildren: Karen and David Ray of Lubbock, and Pamela, Dennis, Randy, and Marla Sue of Elgin.

Mr. D. B. Ray has barbered 50 years, and he and his wife have one daughter, Mrs. May Dell Baskett, and one grandson, Tim, of Elgin.

CONGRATULATIONS, ELGIN, ON YOUR 100 YEARS OF OUTSTANDING PROGRESS! WE ARE PROUD TO HAVE BEEN A PART IN ELGIN'S PROGRESS FOR THE PAST .... SIX YEARS

To the pioneers, whose far-seeing judgment and Christian belief have made Elgin one of the growing and progressive towns of this part of Texas, where families take root and grow, nurtured by working churches, good schools, and expressed neighborliness, we say again, congratulations!

Miller-Newby Funeral Home

Phone 285-4616
Homer, Margaret, and Pam

MOGONYE BROTHERS LUMBER COMPANY

102 N. Ave. C

This business was established originally by Mutual Lumber Company and was managed by Mr. T. J. McClendon. The company was first located where the City Park is now. Around 1912, it was moved to its present location. After Mr. McClendon's death in 1936, his son, Bob, became the manager until the business was purchased by Mogonye Brothers in 1963. Mrs. Gladys McClendon has continued to work with this firm as a most faithful and conscientious bookkeeper.

We at Mogonye Brothers have always been concerned with the growth and development of the community, and we consider it a privilege to serve this trade area. We pledge our service to you, our customers, in Elgin's future.

JOE'S TOGGERY

106 North Main St.

Phone 285-4611

JOE I. DILDY

Oldest Active Elgin Merchant—Nearing His 60th Year

Joe I. Dildy began his retail clothing career in 1912, at the age of 19, when he became an employee of the Poth Dry Goods Co. In 1933, Mr. Dildy left Poth Co. and began his own business under the trade name of Joe's Toggery. This new business was located next to the City Cafe and offered top quality men's clothing in good, standard brands.

In 1942, the business outgrew its small floor space and moved to its present location, 106 North Main Street. Limited ladies wear and household goods were added to offer a more complete inventory.

After four years' service in World War II, Mr. Dildy's son, Harold E. Dildy, joined the firm as a partner. The father-son team still operates the store today and continues to offer standard brand merchandise to its growing Central Texas clientele.

Lee Dildy, grandson of Joe I. Dildy, has become a third generation addition to the firm. Lee divides his time between classes at the University of Texas and the store.

SIMON'S DEPARTMENT STORE

30 North Main

Phone 285-4428

In August, 1919, Mr. and Mrs. H. Simon moved to Elgin from Hempstead, Texas, and opened his Dry Goods and Clothing Store in the old Smith building, the present site of McVay Plumbing and Electric. In 1921, Mr. Simon, assisted by his sons, Abe, Manny, and Meyer, opened a second store two blocks south of the Elgin National Bank. The store was moved to its present location in 1932. Joe Simon purchased the business from his father in 1935. Two years later in 1937, Mr. and Mrs. H. Simon moved to Houston, where Mrs. Simon (Sarah) still resides. Mr .H. Simon passed away in 1941.

Joe and Evelyn Simon, with the capable assistance of John Henry Snowden, who has been in their employ since 1947, strive to serve their customers in Elgin and the surrounding trade area in the best possible manner. Simon's Department Store carries a complete line of fine fashions and famous brand names. Mrs. Fern Cooke and Mrs. John Henry Snowden greet everyone with a smile and try to be helpful to all shoppers.

Q & S GROCERY and MARKET

Quality and Service

Swenson and Lundgren

In 1925, Oscar Swenson and Louis Lundgren formed a partnership and purchased the Q & S Grocery from Carl Walberg. Four years later, they bought the meat market from Walter Maurer to make a complete food store. They operated this business on North Main until 1948. In 1948, they had a fire that destroyed their business, but they were to not be discouraged. They bought the corner of North Main and Taylor Road and built a complete food store, where they have enjoyed a good business.

In 1969, Louis Lundgren, co-owner, passed away. Since this loss, the Q & S Grocery Store has continued as a partnership composed of Oscar Swenson and Louis Lundgren Estate. We sincerely thank the many faithful customers from the Elgin area for their business.

A. E. JOHNSON and SONS, INC.

205 South Main Street - Phone 285-4141

In 1926, A. E. Johnson moved his blacksmith and welding shop to Elgin from Lund and located in the old Samuelson Shop on West 2nd St. In 1935, Mr. Johnson purchased a lot at 111 W. 2nd and built a shop building, which was later enlarged and remodeled. Mr. Johnson later added a machine shop, where cotton poison machines, sweet potato transplanters, and cattle trailers were built. In 1946, Mr. Johnson added a tractor and implement dealership to the business. Mr. Johnson's children, Ruby, Arville, Arbie, and Arthur, were associated with him in the business, and after Mr. Johnson's death in 1955, they continued to operate the business. In 1959, the business changed to manufacturing feed block presses and dump and bagging scales for the feed industry. In 1960, the shop building was sold and the former ice plant building at 205 South Main was purchased, remodeled, and enlarged for the shop. In 1964, hydraulic packers and packaging machines were added to the line of products. The business, now owned and operated by Arville, Arbie, Arthur, and Ruby Johnson Rivers, will celebrate its 50th Anniversary in Elgin in 1976.

THE COURIER HAS BROUGHT
ELGIN'S HISTORICAL STORY
FOR
82 YEARS

Bob Barton, Jr., Publisher
Beverly Williams, Managing Editor
Bessie Dube, Compositor

The Elgin Courier

108 West First
Phone 285-4200

UPCHURCH DRUG STORE

"Serving Elgin and Vicinity for 42 Years"

Harvey Upchurch started in business in 1930, with a newstand and house to house delivery of five daily newspapers. Delivery was made from a "Model T" Ford. The addition of school supplies and stationery was the next growth. The business was then located in Dr. Wood's building. In 1934, Mr. Upchurch purchased a soda fountain and all accessories from W. H. (Bill) Nairn for the sum of $250.00. The business was moved to the building now occupied by Simon's Department Store. In the summer of 1939, the business was again moved, this time to its present location. A gift shop was added to the store and in January, 1954, a pharmacy was opened, also. On April 15, 1957, the store was completely destroyed by fire. A new building was constructed and in September, 1957, the new, modern building was opened. Keeping abreast of the times, Upchurch's was once again remodeled in the summer of 1971.

"A TRIBUTE TO HARVEY AND SARAH UPCHURCH"

Forty years of service to the citizens of Elgin

For many years, "Upchurch's", or as it was commonly referred to as "Harvey's", was the hub of Elgin's every activity. Every day began and ended at Upchurch's. From 6 a.m. to 8 a.m., Elgin businessmen had their morning coffee and chatted. The scene was repeated at 10 a.m. and at 3 p.m. coffee breaks. The young adults gathered each evening from 7 p.m. until 11 p.m. At other times, there were Saturday morning quarterbacks, courters on the old couch and young people reading funny books or grazing on the candies. Who can forget these delights? Upchurch's exemplified the "True American Corner Drug Store".

ARBUCKLE OIL COMPANY

Wholesale Sales and Garage 111 S. Main Phone 285-4701

Service Station 301 S. Main Phone 285-4848

If there is any business firm in Elgin that can claim to be "All Elgin," it is Arbuckle Oil Company, now the Arco Commission Agent and Goodyear Dealer. The Arbuckles are truly home-grown: Mr. Wallace Arbuckle's father was born and reared near Hogeye, Texas, and he can trace his family back to the British Isles. Mr. Arbuckle was born and educated in Elgin, as were his two sons, W. E., Jr., and Ronny.

The business was founded in May, 1931, when Mr. Wallace Arbuckle opened the Arbuckle Service Station and Garage. In 1934, the name was changed to Arbuckle Oil Company, when Mr. Arbuckle became the Sinclair Commission Agent, serving other stations, farms, and ranches in the area. In 1955, W. E. Arbuckle, Jr., joined his father in the business, and in 1958, Mr. Arbuckle's other son, Ronny, also joined the firm.

Arbuckle Oil Company has two trucks which handle bulk delivery to service stations, farms, and ranches. There are two tire trucks available for on-the-road service. The garage offers general auto repair and brake work, motor rebuilding, and sells auto parts, wholesale and retail. Arbuckle Oil Company has won several sales awards from both Arco and Goodyear, all because of their outstanding sales performance records in the Southern District of Texas.

All the Arbuckles are active in civic and church affairs. When asked for comments on their years of business in Elgin, they all expressed gratitude to their many faithful customers and said that Elgin has been good to them.

ELGIN INSURANCE AGENCY

James Cartwright

115 West 2nd

Phone 285-3233

During this, Elgin's Centennial Year, the Elgin Insurance Agency, owned by Mr. James Cartwright, will celebrate its fifteenth year of service to Elgin. The Elgin Insurance Agency represents a consolidation, over the years, of the King Agency, the Culp Agency, the Dannelley Agency, and the Whitten-Fromme Agency. Through these agencies of the past years and Mr. Cartwright's present agency, the Hartford Insurance Group has been represented here in Elgin since 1922 and observes its fiftieth anniversary of service to the people of Elgin this year.

Luther E. Lundgren—Used Cars

203 North Main - Phone 285-4110

In 1922, Luther E. Lundgren began selling cars for Fromme Motor Company at a salary of $50.00 per month. In 1929, Mr. Lundgren became an employee of Keeble Chevrolet Company, where he sold the first six cylinder car bought in Bastrop County. In 1937, Mr. Lundgren joined the staff of Rivers' Chevrolet Company, where he remained until 1952, when he began working for Gruetzner Chevrolet Company, for whom he has worked 20 years. Out of the 49 years Mr. Lundgren has been selling cars, he has completed the Legion of Leaders Sales Contest requirements 33 years. Martinez when he began making platinum resistance temperature sensors

In photo: Mr. Lundgren, left, 1911 Krit Motor Car, which Mr. Lundgren sold to Mr. Charles Mann, right, of Tucson, Arizona.

ALBERT MIKULENCAK
105 North Main Street
Elgin, Texas 78621

In photo, l. to r.: Mr. and Mrs. Albert Mikulencak, Bernard Mikulencak, Mr. and Mrs. Frank J. Mikulencak, Jr. Seated: Mr. and Mrs. F. J. Mikulencak, Sr.

THE MIKULENCAK STORY

Mr. and Mrs. Albert Mikulencak moved to Elgin and opened the Mikulencak's Variety Store on February 12, 1941, after buying the Lawrence Necessity Store. Mikulencak is the son of Mr. and Mrs. F. J. Mikulencak, Sr., and his wife is the daughter of Mr. and Mrs. Frank Hajda, all of Granger. Mikulencak's father opened the first store of the present five store chain in 1924. In 1948, Albert Mikulencak bought the Curling Necessity Store in Bartlett. In 1955 his two brothers, Frank, Jr. and Bernard, bought out their father and the Bartlett store from their brother, Albert, and also purchased a store in Thorndale. In 1953, Mikulencak bought the Hirsh buildings at 105-107 North Main and completely renovated the two buildings. A new Ben Franklin store was opened in 1954. In 1958, the original store was moved to 105 North Main and became known as Mikulencak's Dry Goods. Mikulencak's parents are now retired and live in Granger. The five Mikulencak stores are still in operation.

The Mikulencaks had six children: Albert, Jr., Dorothy, Alice, and Daniel and Ann (twins who died in infancy), and Barbara. Mrs. Mikulencak was manager of Ben Franklin for seven years and has been manager of the store since it became known as Franklin's in 1961.

WESTERN AUTO ASSOCIATE STORE

N. P. Worthey, Owner

108-110 North Main Street Phone 285-3212

In April, 1945, Mr. and Mrs. N. P. Worthey and their children, Ardeth and Richard, moved to Elgin from Houston. On April 15 of that same year, Mr. Worthey opened his Western Auto Associate Store in the M. L. Rivers grocery store building, where it remained for three years. At this time, Mr. Worthey employed one person. In March, 1948, Mr. Worthey moved his store into half of the C. A. Sandahl building on Main Street. By 1953, the business had grown to the point where Mr. Worthey needed more room. Therefore, when Mrs. Sandahl offered a lease on the whole building, Mr. Worthey accepted and moved into the half of the building formerly occupied by Kiecke Auto Supply, as well as the half already occupied by Western Auto Associate Store. In 1959, Mr. Worthey purchased the building from Mrs. Sandahl. The Worthey's son, Richard, came into the business in 1954 and now, Richard's son, Michael, a student at Elgin High School, works part-time at the store. During the past 27 years, Mr. Worthey's business has grown steadily, until at the present time, he employs six people.

YOUNG WORLD

117 North Main Street
Phone 285-4939

Large enough to serve you—
small enough to know you.

FOUNDED IN ELGIN'S
CENTENNIAL YEAR

JERRY'S BEAUTY SHOP

Jerry Terrell, Owner
116 North Main Street
Phone 285-3244

SERVING THE LADIES OF ELGIN FOR THE PAST SEVEN YEARS

POP'S PLACE

August Weisner, Manager

MAY WE ALL BENEFIT FROM ELGIN'S HISTORY, SO AS TO PROSPER IN THE FUTURE

RAMSEY PHARMACY

115 North Main

Phone 285-3838

Mr. and Mrs. Charles Ramsey came to Elgin in 1946, and established their business in the old McLeod Pharmacy, which was located on Main Street. The store was located there for 4 years until 1950, when it was moved to its present location, 115 North Main Street. Ramsey Pharmacy has served the needs of the people of Elgin for 26 years, offering fountain service, cosmetics, stationery, papers and magazines, patent medicines, and complete pharmacy service.

GRUETZNER CHEVROLET COMPANY

1131 N. Highway 290

Otto Gruetzner bought the existing Chevrolet dealership on Friday, June 13, 1952. The business was located then at 404 North Main Street. Working with Mr. Gruetzner was Otto Gruetzner, Jr., Bobby Gruetzner, Luther Lundgren, and Earl Ray Glover. In 1953, the business relocated at 200 North Main, at which time the building was remodeled and August (Uce) Gruetzner joined the business. The dealership remained at this location until 1962, when the existing plant was built at 1131 North Highway 290. The firm employs approximately 20 people and is presently under an expansion program to accomodate the growing needs of the growing Elgin community.

THE SAM MECEYS

We have lived in Elgin since 1945. In 1954 Sam became a distributor with Falstaff Brewing Corporation. We added Miller High Life Beer to our distributorship in 1965. In June, 1968, we built a new warehouse at 207 West Austin Street, from which we service Bastrop County.

We extend our thanks to all of our customers who have helped our business to proper in the past and we hope to serve you in the future!

Sam and Faye Mecey

OUR FUTURE, AS DID OUR PAST, DEPENDS ON YOU,

THE CUSTOMER

COMPLIMENTS

OF

GREENLINE CHEMICAL COMPANY

Highway 95

Phone 285-3343

I. G. Janca, Owner

Patrick's Texaco Station
Highway 290

HAPPY 100th
ANNIVERSARY,
ELGIN!

Margaret's Beauty Shop
Serving the Beauty Needs of the Ladies of Elgin Since 1932.

Jo Nell   Mary Ann
Jean   Lana
Margaret Craig

BRAZOS TRAIL SADDLERY
411 South Highway 290
Phone 285-4683

Brazos Trail Saddlery opened in May, 1968 in what had been a small contractor's offiice located on Highway 290 at Alamo Street. Horse supplies, boots, and hats were featured in the limited facility. In June, 1969, a Grand Opening featured a newly constructed 3200 square foot building. The store's inventory was expanded to include ladies and children's wear.
Brazos Trail Saddlery is proud to be a part of the Elgin Community and looks forward to serving the people of Elgin in the future.

Carl K. Nygard
Collector of
Colt Firearms, Gold Coins,
and
National Bank Currency
Buy, Sell, or Trade

Route 4, Box 166 Elgin, Texas
Phone 285-4858

GRASS PLANTING
Coastal, Coast Cross #1, and
Zimmerly Select

FRESH ROOTS ALWAYS

Jarmon Wiley
801 North Main Street
Phone 285-3353

SOUTH SIDE MARKET
AND BAR-B-QUE

THE ORIGINAL ELGIN
HOT
SAUSAGE

SOUTH SIDE MARKET
FOUNDED OVER EIGHTY
YEARS AGO

Owners
Mr. & Mrs. Ernest W.
Bracewell, Sr.

Dr. Warner's

CHIROPRACTIC CLINIC

Phone 285-4105

Dr. S. T. Warner graduated from Texas Chiropractic College, San Antonio, Texas, now located in Pasadena, Texas, and has practiced as a Chiropractor in Elgin for nearly 23 years. First, Dr. Warner was located in Charles Zegub's property across from Miller-Newby Mortuary and later at 700 North Avenue C. Still later, needing more room, Dr. Warner bought the property at 113 West Seventh Street, where his Chiropractic Clinic is located. Dr. and Mrs. Warner have many very good friends whom they have learned to know since moving to Elgin in 1949.

ELGIN LUMBER COMPANY

301 North Main
Phone 285-3202

THE GROWTH AND ECONOMY OF ELGIN HAS CHANGED A GREAT DEAL IN THE PAST CENTURY. WE HOPE TO CONTINUE TO SERVE ELGIN AS IT CONTINUES TO CHANGE IN THE FUTURE.

Heine Heidig

ELGIN GRAIN & FEED COMPANY, INC.

Feed Manufacturers

P. O. Box 586

Phone 285-3344

This firm began manufacturing a complete line of livestock feeds in 1960. The line includes range cubes, dairy feed, and hog feed. We are also manufacturers of mineral blocks, protein blocks, and horse blocks.

1872 **ELGIN** **1972**

CENTENNIAL

We are proud to have been a part of Elgin the past thirty-four years. It is a fine community in which to raise your family!

To the people of this community and to the Texaco Dealers, we want to express our appreciation of continuous association as your Texaco, Incorporated consignee.

Charles P. Morrison

Mrs. Charles P. Morrison

SUTTON'S GULF SERVICE STATION
1121 N. Highway 290
Phone 285-9326

The growth and development of Elgin has always been our main concern in the past and will continue to be in the future.

Virgle and Marjorie Sutton

O. L. ALMQUIST FEED AND SEED

107 North Ave. E

Phone 285-4437

Our future, as did our past, depends on you, the customer. May we continue to serve you.

It has been a privilege to have been a part of Elgin for over 50 years—with some interruptions—and I still like to call it "Home."

Guy Carter

Nash Station and Grocery

Highway 290
Phone 285-4116
We are proud of Elgin's heritage and interested in its future.

Allie Nash

Stop'N Shop

Grocery and Bar-B-Que

Highway 290

Phone 285-3402

Elgin, we wish for you in the next 100 years as much advancement as in the last 100 years.

JONES GROCERY

619 Beaukiss Lane
Phone 285-3511

Serving the Elgin Community Since 1945

For more than 23 years, satisfied Elgin customers have used Hoffman Paints. We are proud to have a wonderful dealer in Elgin:

MOGONYE BROS.

LUMBER COMPANY

Construction on the building at 116 North Main Street, owned by Mr. Otto Bengtson, was begun on November 23, 1912, and completed in 1913. The building has housed, through the years, Sellstrom Hardware Co., Sam Culp Hardware Co., and Red & White Grocery. The ownership of the building remained in the Bengtson family until November 20, 1971, when it was purchased by Mr. Charley Smith, owner of The Fabric Shop. The building now houses The Fabric Shop and Jerry's Beauty Shop.
We are happy to be a part of Elgin's growth!

THE FABRIC SHOP

116 North Main Street

The building at 104 North Main Street was built in the early 1900s and was purchased in 1965 by Harold E. Dildy. The building was remodeled and leased to Mrs. Charley Smith and Mrs. Tom Rankin. The two ladies opened a dress shop, named Dor-Leen's Ladies Wear.

Congratulations to Elgin
on 100 years of progress!

DOR-LEEN'S

104 North Main Street

CONGRATULATIONS!

THE RETZLAFFS

ARNOLD WANDA

WEED INSTRUMENT CO., INC.

The company was started in 1967 as a single proprietorship by Rudy Martinez when he began making platinum resistance temperature sensors in his kitchen in California. In April of 1967 he returned to his native San Antonio, Texas, to begin his business in earnest.

The business was incorporated as Weed Instrument Company, Inc. in January, 1968, by a small group of investors in San Antonio. In August of 1968, J. J. Moore joined Weed as an investor-stockholder and a consultant in physics, electronics, and management. The company continued to manufacture platinum resistance sensors and the proprietary techniques were refined for adaptation to large scale production of quality sensors.

In early 1969 a planned marketing and advertising program was begun. Literature was designed and printed, and a network of manufacturer-representatives was started. In April, 1969, the plant was moved to Elgin. During the summer a direct mail campaign was begun using a newly printed brochure describing the products. WEED exhibited at the Instrument Society of America Show & Exhibit at Houston in October, 1969, and made many new contacts. They also discovered that they were already developing a good image.

During late 1969, electronic temperature instrumentation was developed to begin a diversification into temperature instrumentation as well as sensors.

WEED presently manufactures platinum resistance temperature sensors and a growing line of electronic instruments for temperature measurement and indication. New types of models of sensors are continually being developed to customers specifications and additional new electronic instrumentation is in the development stage.

Any user who needs to measure temperature of liquids, gases, or solids accurately, reliably and repeatedly is a potential customer of WEED. This includes the following industries: Hydrocarbon Processing (Petroleum Refining and Petrochemicals), Food Processing, Pulp and Paper, Plastics, Chemicals, Electric Power, Artificial Fibres, Shipbuilding and Marine Shipping, Pollution Control, Oceanography, Aerospace, and Military Research and Development.

TEXAS POWER & LIGHT CO.

25 North Main

Phone 285-4033

Texas Power & Light Company began serving the city of Elgin with electric power on December 6, 1926.

TP&L purchased the Elgin electric properties from the Texas Public Utilities, which had acquired the system in December, 1925, from E. A. Clousnitzer.

When TP&L began service here, there were 11 miles of distribution lines and 530 electric customers. The population of Elgin at that time was approximately 1,825.

In 1926, electric service in the area was bolstered. First, a 60,000-volt transmission line was constructed from the Williamson County line to Elgin, Bastrop, San Marcos, and Hunter. The line extended for a total of 74 miles.

Secondly, a 12,500-volt line was constructed from Elgin to the Elgin Brick Plant and on to McDade. This line extended 10 miles. At the time TP&L purchased the Elgin facilities, Texas Public Utilities owned a number of properties in the area, consisting of electric, gas, water, and ice facilities. Most were located in the TP&L service area. The sale was made to TP&L in the interest of operating economy.

www.ingramcontent.com/pod-product-compliance
Lightning Source LLC
LaVergne TN
LVHW010616100826
845148LV00014B/2997
9781681793801